John tells us the Good News about Jesus

Bible Society
Trinity Business Centre
Stonehill Green, Westlea
Swindon SN5 7DG
biblesociety.org.uk
bibleresources.org.uk

EasyEnglish Gospel of John
ISBN 978-0-564-04973-8

Typography and typesetting by Bible Society Resources Ltd,
a wholly-owned subsidiary of The British and Foreign Bible Society

EEGJ/BSR/2015

CONTENTS

John tells us the Good News about Jesus

A word list at the end explains words with a star* by them

About this book

John's Gospel is one of the four Gospels. 'Gospel' means 'good news'. The Gospels are the books that tell us about Jesus' life on earth. John was one of the three disciples* who knew the LORD Jesus Christ best. John called himself 'the disciple* that Jesus loved'. We think that John wrote his Gospel in the city called Ephesus. He wrote it some years after Matthew, Mark and Luke wrote their Gospels. He wrote it about 70 years after Christ's birth.

John's Gospel is different from the other three Gospels. It does not describe many things that the Gospels of Matthew, Mark and Luke do describe. But it does include many things that are not in the other Gospels. John tells us much more about who Jesus was. John shows us Jesus as the Son of God – the only person who can cause us to live. John teaches us more about God's Spirit, too.

At the beginning of his Gospel, John calls Jesus 'the Word'.

JOHN

1

The Word became human

[1]In the beginning, the Word was already there. The Word
was with God. The Word was God. [2]He was with God in the
beginning. [3]God made all things by the Word. God did not
make anything without him. [4]It is the Word who causes us to
live. And because of this, he was the light to all people. [5]The
light shines in the dark, and the dark cannot put out the light.

[6]God sent a man. His name was John. [7]He came to tell people
about the light. God wanted everyone to believe what John
said. [8]John himself was not that light. God sent him to tell
people about the light. [9]The true light, that gives light to
every person, was coming into the world.

[10]The Word was in the world. God made the world by him. But
the world did not know who he was. [11]He came to what was
his own. But his own people did not accept him. [12]But some
people did accept him. Some people did believe who he was. So,
he gave authority to those people so that they could become
God's children. [13]These children were not born in the usual
human way. They were not born because of what any people
wanted. They were not born because of what any man decided.
No! They were born from God. [14]The Word became human. He
lived among us. We saw how great and how good he is. He is
great and good as only the Father's one true Son can be. He is
completely kind. He is full of what is true.

[15]John told people about the Word. He shouted, 'This is the
man that I told you about. He comes after me. But he is

greater than I am. He was there before I was born.' 16The
Word is full of everything that we need. All of us have received
from him. We have received one good thing after another
good thing. 17God gave his rules by Moses. But God has been
kind to us by Jesus Christ. God has brought his true message
to us by Jesus Christ. 18No person has ever seen God. But
God's only true Son, who is so very near to the Father, has
shown God to us.

John the Baptist* was not Christ*

19The Jews'* leaders sent priests* and Levites* from
Jerusalem to ask John, 'Who are you?' This is what he said.
20John did not refuse to answer. He said, 'I am not the Christ*.'
21So they asked him, 'So who are you? Are you Elijah?' John
said, 'No, I am not.' They asked, 'Are you the Prophet*?' John
answered, 'No.' 22Then they said, 'Tell us who you are. We
must say something to the people who sent us. What do you
say about yourself?' 23He said, 'I am the voice that shouts in
the wild places*. I shout, "Make a straight path for the LORD
to come." That is what the prophet* Isaiah said.' 24The men
who came to ask these questions were Pharisees*. 25They said
to John, 'Why do you baptise* people, if you are neither the
Christ* nor Elijah nor the Prophet*?'

26John replied, 'I baptise* people with water. But there is
someone here among you that you do not know. 27It is he
who comes after me. I am not good enough even to take off
his shoes.' 28All these things happened at a place east from
the Jordan river. It was a village called Bethany. John was
baptising* people there.

29The next day, John saw Jesus, who was coming towards him.
John said, 'Look! Here is God's Lamb (young sheep), who takes
away the world's sin*. 30This is the man that I told you about.
I told you, "It is he who comes after me. But he is greater
than I am. He was already there before I was born." 31I did
not know him. But I had to show Israel's people who he was.
That is why I am baptising* people with water.' 32John told

them, 'I saw God's Spirit come down from the sky. He came
like a dove (a kind of bird) and he stayed on Jesus. 33 I would
not have known who Jesus was. But God had sent me to
baptise* people with water. And God told me, "You will see the
Spirit come down. He will stay on someone. That is the person
who will baptise* people with my Holy (completely good)
Spirit." 34 Now I have seen this. So, I can tell you that this is
God's Son.'

Jesus' first disciples*

35 John and two of his disciples* were standing there the next
day. 36 John saw Jesus, who was walking past them. John said,
'Look! There is God's Lamb (young sheep).' 37 When the two
disciples* heard this, they followed Jesus. 38 Then Jesus turned
round. He saw that they were following him. He asked them,
'What do you want?' They said, 'Rabbi (which means Teacher),
where are you staying?' 39 Jesus replied, 'Come, and you will
see.' So, they went with him. And they saw where he was
staying. It was about 10 in the morning. And they stayed with
him that day.

40 Andrew was one of the two disciples* who had followed
Jesus. They had heard what John had said about Jesus.
Andrew was Simon Peter's brother. 41 The first thing that
Andrew did was to find his brother, Simon. Andrew said to
Simon, 'We have found the Messiah*.' (Messiah means Christ*.)
42 Then he brought Simon to Jesus. Jesus looked at Simon and
he said, 'You are Simon, John's son. Your name will be Cephas.'
This name is the same as Peter, which means 'rock'.

43 The next day, Jesus decided to go to Galilee. He met Philip,
and Jesus said to Philip, 'Follow me.' 44 Philip, like Andrew and
Peter, came from the town called Bethsaida. 45 Philip went
to find Nathanael. He told Nathanael, 'We have found the
man that Moses wrote about in the book of God's rules. The
prophets* wrote about him, too. He is Jesus, who is Joseph's
son, from Nazareth.' 46 Nathanael said, 'I did not think that

anything good could come from Nazareth!' Philip replied, 'Come and see.'

47 Jesus saw Nathanael, who was coming towards him. Jesus said, 'Here is a completely honest man. That is what a person from Israel should really be like.' 48 Nathanael asked, 'How do you know me?' Jesus answered, 'I saw you before Philip asked you to come. I saw you when you were under the fig (fruit) tree.' 49 Nathanael said, 'Teacher, you are the Son of God. You are the King of Israel.' 50 Jesus said to him, 'I told you that I saw you under the fig (fruit) tree. And you believe me because I told you that. But you will see much greater things than that.' 51 And Jesus said to him, 'I am telling you what is true. You will see heaven (the sky) open. You will see God's angels*. They will be going up and they will be coming down on the Son of Man.'

2

The marriage at Cana

1 Two days after that, there was a marriage. It was in the town called Cana, in Galilee. Jesus' mother was there. 2 People had asked Jesus and his disciples* to come to the party also. 3 When people had drunk all the wine*, Jesus' mother said to him, 'They have no more wine*.' 4 Jesus replied, 'Woman, why do you tell me this? It is not my time yet.' 5 His mother said to the servants, 'Do anything that he wants you to do.'

6 There were 6 big pots there, which people had made from stone. Each pot could contain 20 to 30 gallons of water. These pots contained water so that the Jews* could wash themselves. The Jews* had special rules about when they must wash themselves. 7 Jesus said to the servants, 'Fill the pots with water.' So they filled the pots to the top. 8 Then he said, 'Now take some of the water from the pots and give it to the master of the party.' So they took the water. 9 And the master of the party tasted the water. But the water had become wine*. The master did not know where the wine* had come from. But the

servants who had given it to him knew. Then the master asked
the bridegroom (the man who had just married) to come to
him. 10The master said to him, 'Everyone else brings out the
best wine* first. Then, when people have had plenty to drink,
they give people cheaper wine*. But you are different. You
have kept the best wine* until now.'

11Jesus did this first miracle* at Cana, in Galilee. In this way,
Jesus showed how great and how powerful he was. Then his
disciples* believed him.

Jesus goes to God's Great House (the temple)

12After this, Jesus went to Capernaum. His mother, his
brothers and his disciples* went with him. They stayed there
for a few days.

13It was almost time for the Jews'* Passover*. So, Jesus went
to Jerusalem. 14In God's Great House (the temple), he found
people who were selling cows, sheep and doves (a kind of
bird). Other people were sitting at tables. They were buying
and selling coins there. 15So Jesus made a whip* from some
pieces of rope*. Then he caused all the people to run out of
God's Great House, with the sheep and the cows. He threw all
the money-changers'* coins on to the ground and he turned
their tables over. 16He said to the people who sold birds, 'Take
them out of here! Do not make my Father's house into a
market!' 17His disciples* remembered what it says in the Old
Testament*: 'My love for your house burns inside me like a fire.'

18Then the Jews* asked Jesus, 'If you have authority to do this,
show us a miracle*. Then we will know that you really do have
authority.' 19Jesus answered them, 'If you destroy this house
of God, I will build it up again in 3 days.' 20The Jews* replied,
'A lot of men worked for 46 years to build this house. And you
say that you will build it in 3 days all by yourself!' 21But the
house that Jesus was speaking about was his own body. 22The
disciples* remembered this when Jesus had become alive again
after his death. They remembered that he had said this. Then

they believed the Old Testament*. And they believed the words
that Jesus had spoken.

23 While Jesus was in Jerusalem for the Passover*, he did many
miracles*. Many people saw these miracles*. As a result, they
believed who Jesus is. 24 But Jesus himself did not trust* the
people. He knew what all people are really like. 25 He did not
need anyone to tell him what people are like. He knew already
what was really in all people.

3

Jesus and Nicodemus

1 There was a Pharisee* called Nicodemus. He was one of the
Jews'* leaders. 2 He came to Jesus at night. He said to Jesus,
'Rabbi (teacher), we know that God has sent you to us. We
have seen the miracles* that you are doing. Nobody could do
these things unless God was with him.' 3 Jesus replied, 'I am
telling you what is true. Unless a person is born from above,
they cannot see God's kingdom*.' 4 Nicodemus asked, 'How
can a man be born when he is old? He cannot return into
his mother's body. He cannot be born a second time.' 5 Jesus
explained, 'I am telling you what is true. Unless a person is
born by water and by God's Spirit, he cannot go into God's
kingdom*. 6 Human people give birth to what is human. But
God's Spirit gives birth to spirit*. 7 I said to you, "You must
be born from above." What I said should not surprise you.
8 Everyone who is born by God's Spirit is like the wind. The
wind blows where it wants. You can hear it. But you cannot
say where it came from. And you cannot say where it is going.'

9 Nicodemus asked, 'How can this happen?' 10 Jesus replied,
'You are a teacher in Israel. You ought to understand these
things! 11 I am telling you what is true. We speak about things
that we know. We tell you what we have seen. But even then,
you people do not believe our words. 12 I have told you about
things that happen in this world. And you do not believe me.
But I am telling you about things that happen in heaven*. So,

I do not think that you will ever believe me about those things.
13 The Son of Man came down from heaven*. Nobody else
has gone up to heaven* except him. 14 And people will lift up
the Son of Man, as Moses lifted up the snake in the wild, dry
place*. Moses made a snake out of metal and he held it up to
show it to Israel's people. In the same way, people will lift up
the Son of Man for everyone to see. 15 As a result, everyone
who believes him will be able to live always. 16 God loved the
people in the world so much that he gave his one and only Son
on their behalf. So, as a result, everyone who believes in the
Son will not die. Instead, they will live always.'

17 God did not send his Son into the world because he wanted
to punish* people. No, God sent his Son to save the people
in the world. 18 God will not decide to punish* anyone who
believes the Son. But God has already decided that he must
punish* some people. Some people refuse to believe who his
one and only Son is. God must punish* anyone who refuses to
believe that. 19 This is why God has already decided to punish*
some people. It is because light has come into the world. But
people did not love the light. They loved the dark instead. That
was because they were doing bad things. 20 Everyone who does
bad things hates* the light. A person like that will not come to
the light because he is afraid. He does not want everyone to
see that he has done bad things. 21 But every person who obeys
everything true comes to the light. So then the light will show
that he was doing God's work. Everyone can see that he was
obeying God.

Jesus and John the Baptist*

22 After this, Jesus and his disciples* went to the country
places in Judea. Jesus stayed there with his disciples* for
some time, and they baptised* people there. 23 John was
baptising* people too. He was at Aenon near Salim because
there was a lot of water there. People were coming to him and
John was baptising* them. 24 (This was before the rulers put
John in a prison.) 25 A certain Jew* began to argue with John's

disciples*. They were arguing about some rules. Those rules
told people when and how they should wash. 26The disciples*
came to John. They said to him, 'Teacher, remember the man,
Jesus, that you spoke to us about. He was with you on the
other side of the Jordan river. Now he is baptising* people and
everyone is going to him.'

27John replied, 'A man can receive only what God gives to him.
28You yourselves will remember what I said. I said, "I am not
the Christ*, but God sent me before the Christ*." 29The bride
(woman who is marrying) is the bridegroom's (man who is
marrying her). But the bridegroom's friend stands near him
and he listens. That friend is very happy when he hears the
bridegroom's voice. I am like that friend, so I am completely
happy now. 30He must become greater, but I must become
less important.

31He who comes from above is greater than all things.
A person who comes from the earth belongs to the earth.
A person like that speaks only about things that belong to
the earth. He who comes from heaven* is greater than all
things. 32He tells what he has seen. He tells what he has heard.
But nobody believes what he is saying. 33Anyone who does
believe his message has said, "Yes, God is true." 34He that
God has sent speaks God's words. God fills him completely
with God's Spirit. 35The Father loves the Son. He has given the
Son authority over all things. 36Anyone who believes the Son
is alive for always. But anyone who will not obey the Son will
never really live. God will continue to be angry with a person
who refuses to obey the Son.'

4

Jesus talks to a woman from Samaria

1The Pharisees* heard the news that many people were
joining Jesus' group of disciples*. They heard that Jesus
was baptising* more disciples* than John. 2(But really Jesus
himself did not baptise* anyone. It was only Jesus' disciples*

who baptised* people.) 3 So, when the LORD knew about this, he
left Judea. He returned to Galilee. 4 On his way, Jesus had to
go through Samaria.

5 He came to a town in Samaria called Sychar. It was near
to the piece of land that Jacob had given to his son, Joseph,
many years earlier. 6-8 Jacob's well was there. Jesus was tired
after his journey. He sat down by the well. It was about 6 in
the evening. His disciples* had gone to buy food in the town.
A woman from Samaria came to the well because she wanted
to get some water. Jesus said to her, 'Give a drink to me.'
9 The woman from Samaria said to him, 'You are a Jew* and
I am a woman from Samaria. Why do you ask me for a drink?'
(The Jews* will not usually even talk to people who belong to
Samaria.)

10 Jesus answered the woman, 'You do not know what God can
give. I asked you to give a drink to me. But you do not know
who I am. If you did know, you would have asked me to give
a drink to you. Then I would have given water to you that
would cause you to live.' 11 The woman said, 'Sir, you have no
bucket, and the well is deep. Where can you get this water
that would cause me to live? 12 Jacob, our ancestor*, gave this
well to us. He, his sons, and his sheep and goats and cows
all drank its water. Are you saying that you are greater than
Jacob?' 13 Jesus answered, 'Everyone who drinks from this
well will get thirsty* again. 14 But I can give a different kind
of water. Whoever drinks that kind of water will never get
thirsty* again. The water that I will give to him will become
a well inside him. That well will continue to give fresh water
that will cause him to live always.' 15 The woman said to him,
'Sir, give this water to me. Then I will never get thirsty* again.
And I will not have to continue to come here so that I can
get water.'

16 Jesus said to her, 'Go, fetch your husband. Then return
here.' 17 The woman replied, 'I have no husband.' Jesus said to
her, 'You are right when you say, "I have no husband." 18 The
fact is that you have had 5 husbands. And now you live with

a man who is not your husband. What you have said is quite
true.' [19]The woman said to him, 'Sir, I can see that you are
a prophet*. [20]Our ancestors* worshipped* on this mountain.
But you Jews* say that Jerusalem is the right place to
worship* God.'

[21]Jesus spoke to her with authority, 'Believe me, woman. Soon
you will not worship* the Father either on this mountain or at
Jerusalem. [22]You people from Samaria do not really know what
you worship*. But we Jews* do know what we worship*. The
way that God has made to save people comes from the Jews*.
[23]But soon, people will really worship* the Father. Really, it is
that time already. Those people who really want to worship*
the Father will worship* him from their spirits*. The Father
looks for people who will worship* him like that. [24]God is
spirit*. Those people who worship* him must worship* from
their spirits*. They must really want to worship* God.' [25]The
woman said to Jesus, 'I know that the Messiah* will come. He
is called Christ. When he comes, he will explain everything to
us.' [26]Then Jesus replied, 'I, who am speaking to you, am he.'

The disciples* return

[27]At this moment, his disciples* returned. They were surprised
to see that Jesus was talking to a woman. But none of them
asked him, 'What do you want?' or, 'Why are you talking to
her?' [28]Then the woman left her water-pot and she returned
to the town. She said to the people there, [29]'Come! See a man
who told me everything about myself. He told me all the things
that I have ever done! He must be the Christ*!' [30]So they left
the town and they went to find Jesus.

[31]While the woman was away, the disciples* said to Jesus,
'Teacher, eat something.' [32]But he said to them, 'I have
food that I can eat. But you do not know about it.' [33]So the
disciples* asked each other, 'Could someone have brought
food to him?' [34]Jesus said to them, 'I must obey him who sent
me. I must finish the work that he has given to me to do. That
is my food. [35]You say, "The plants in the farmers' fields will

be ready for the harvest* after 4 more months." But I say
that you should open your eyes. Look at the fields. The plants
are ready for the harvest now. 36 God is paying the workers
already. They are bringing in the fruit. They are bringing in
people who will live always. The person who plants the seeds
will be very happy. And the person who brings in the fruit will
be very happy too. Both of them will be happy as a result of
their work. 37 What people say is true. One person plants the
seeds and another person brings in the fruit. 38 I sent you to
fetch people like fruit that you have not worked for. Other
people did the work. You have brought in the fruit (people)
that they worked for.'

39 Many of the people who lived in that town in Samaria heard
the woman's story. She had said to them, 'He told me all
the things that I have ever done!' And because of this, they
believed Jesus. 40 So when these people from Samaria came
to Jesus, they asked him to stay with them. And he stayed
there for two more days. 41 Many more people believed Jesus
when they listened to his own words. 42 The people said to the
woman, 'Now we believe him because we ourselves have heard
him. Now we do not believe only because of what you said.
This man really is the man who will save the world. We know
that now.'

Jesus makes an officer's son well

43 After two days, Jesus left there and he went to Galilee.
44 (Jesus himself had said earlier, 'When a prophet* visits
places near his own home, the people there never believe
him. The people there never think that a prophet* from their
place could be important.') 45 When he arrived in Galilee, the
people there were happy to see him. They had been at the
Passover* also. And they had seen all the things that he had
done at Jerusalem.

46 Jesus visited Cana, in Galilee, again. This was the town
where he had changed the water into wine*. A certain man
who was one of the king's officers was there. This officer

had a son who was at Capernaum. His son was very ill. 47 This
man had heard the news that Jesus had arrived in Galilee
from Judea. So, he went to Jesus. He asked Jesus to go to
Capernaum, where the man's son was dying. He asked Jesus
strongly to make his son well. 48 Then Jesus said to him, 'You
people want me to do great miracles* that will surprise you.
Unless you see these great miracles*, none of you will ever
believe.' 49 The king's officer said to Jesus, 'Sir, come with me
now before my child dies.' 50 Jesus replied, 'Go home. Your
son will live.' The man believed what Jesus had said. And
he started to go home. 51 While he was travelling home, his
servants met him. They told him, 'Your boy will live.' 52 He
asked them, 'At what time did he start to get well?' They
told him, 'He stopped being ill yesterday, at 7 in the evening.'
53 Then the father remembered that time. It was the time when
Jesus had spoken to him. It was when Jesus had said, 'Your
son will live.' So, the man and all his family believed. 54 This
was the second miracle* that Jesus did after he returned from
Judea to Galilee.

5

Jesus makes a man able to walk

1 Some time after that, Jesus went to Jerusalem, because it
was time for one of the Jews'* festivals*.

2 There is a pool near the Sheep Gate in Jerusalem. Its name
in the Jews'* language is Bethesda. Round the pool, there is
a building with 5 places that have a roof over them. 3 A large
number of sick people were lying in these places. Some of
them could not see. Some of them could not walk. Some of
them could not move themselves properly. They were waiting
for when the water started to move. 4 An angel* went down
into the pool at certain times and he moved the water. Then
all the sick people tried to get into the pool. The first person
who got into the water became well. That person became well,
whatever his illness was.

5 One man there had been ill for 38 years. 6 Jesus saw this man,
who was lying there. Jesus knew that the man had been ill like
this for a very long time. So he asked the man, 'Do you want
to get well?' 7 The sick man said, 'Sir, I do not have anyone
who will help me. I need somebody who will put me into the
pool. When the water starts to move, I try to get in. But
someone else always gets in before me.' 8 Then Jesus said to
him, 'Get up! Pick up your bed and walk.' 9 The man became
well immediately. He picked up his bed and he walked. The day
when this happened was a Sabbath* day.

10 So, the Jews'* leaders spoke to the man that Jesus had made
well. They said to him, 'You must not carry your bed on the
Sabbath* day. You are not obeying the rules.' 11 He replied,
'A man made me well. That man said to me, "Pick up your bed
and walk." ' 12 So they asked him, 'Who is this man? Who said
to you, "Pick up your bed and walk"?' 13 The man that Jesus
had made well did not know. He did not know who it was.
Jesus had gone away into the crowd that was there.

14 Some time after that, Jesus found the man in God's Great
House (the temple). Jesus said to him, 'See, you have become
well. Stop doing wrong things. If you do not stop, something
worse may happen to you.' 15 Then the man went to the Jews'*
leaders. He told them that it was Jesus. It was Jesus who
had made him well. 16 The Jews'* leaders were angry because
Jesus had made a man well on the Sabbath* day. So, they
began to cause a lot of trouble for Jesus. 17 But Jesus said to
them, 'My Father is still working, and I am working too.' 18 So,
because Jesus said this, the Jews'* leaders got even angrier.
They wanted even more to kill him. He not only worked on the
Sabbath* day. He was also calling God his own Father, so he
was making himself equal with God.

19 So, Jesus answered them, 'I am telling you what is true.
The Son can do nothing by himself. He sees what the Father
does. And he can do only those same things. What the Father
does, the Son does also. 20 The Father loves the Son. So, he
shows the Son all the things that he himself does. And the

Father will show the Son even greater things than these.
These greater things will surprise you even more. 21 The
Father raises dead people, to make them alive again. In the
same way, the Son makes alive whoever he chooses. 22 More
than that, the Father does not judge* anyone. He has given
authority to the Son completely so that the Son will judge*
all people. 23 So then all people will know how great the Son
is. They know that the Father is very great. In the same way,
they will know also that the Son is very great. Some people
may refuse to think that the Son is great or important. But
really, those people are thinking the same things about the
Father, because he sent the Son. 24 I am telling you what is
true. Everyone who hears my words should believe the Father.
They should believe him who sent me. If they do believe, they
are alive for always. God will not punish* them because of the
wrong things that they have done. They were dead, but now
they have become alive.'

25 'I am telling you what is true. A time will happen soon when
the dead people will hear the voice of the Son of God. Really,
it is that time already. Those people who hear the Son's voice
will live. 26 The Father himself can cause people to live. In
the same way, he has made the Son able to do this also. The
Son himself can cause people to live. 27 Also, the Father has
given authority to the Son so that he judges* people. The
Son says what is right for each person. That is because he is
the Son of Man. 28 Do not be surprised by this. There will be
a time when all the dead people under the ground will hear
the Son's voice. 29 They will come out from the ground. Those
people who have done good things will rise. They will rise so
that they can live with God always. Those people who have
done bad things will rise. But they will rise so that God can
punish* them.'

Things that show who Jesus really is

30 'I can do nothing by myself. I hear what the Father says to
me. Then, because of what he says, I judge*. So, what I judge*

is right. I am not trying to do what I myself want. The Father
sent me. And I want to do what he wants. 31 If I said great
things about myself, my words would not be true. 32 But there
is someone else who speaks about me. What he says about me
is true. I know that. 33 You have sent your people to ask John
about me. What he has told you about me is true. 34 I do not
need any man to speak on my behalf. No, but I am telling you
this only so that God will be able to save you. 35 John was like a
light that shone brightly. And for a certain time, you enjoyed
the light that he gave.'

36 'But other things show who I am. My Father has given work
to me so that I could finish it. And these things that I do, they
speak about me. They speak more strongly than John's words.
They show that the Father has sent me. 37 Also, the Father
himself, who sent me, has spoken about me. You have never
heard his voice. And you have never seen his shape. 38 His word
does not stay inside you. You do not believe the Person that
the Father sent. That is why his word does not stay in you.
39 You study the Scriptures (Old Testament*) carefully. You
think that they will cause you to live. And the Scriptures (Old
Testament*) themselves tell you about me. 40 But you refuse to
come to me so that you could really live!'

41 'I am not wanting people to say great things about me. If
people say great things about me, that is not important to
me. 42 But I know what kind of people you are. I know that you
do not really love God or other people. 43 I have come with my
Father's authority, but you do not accept me. But if someone
else comes with his own authority, you will accept him. 44 When
you say good things about each other, it makes you happy. But
you do not try to make God happy. You do not want the only
God to say good things about you. That is why you cannot
believe me. 45 But I will not tell the Father that you are wrong.
Do not think that I will do that. No, because it is Moses who
will do that. You hope that Moses will help you. But he will tell
the Father that you are wrong. 46 If you had really believed
Moses, you would have believed me. That is because Moses

wrote about me. 47But you do not believe what Moses wrote.
So, you cannot believe what I say.'

6

Jesus feeds 5000 men and their families

1Some time after that, Jesus went across Lake Galilee, which
is also called Lake Tiberias. 2A large crowd of people followed
him, because of the miracles* that he had done. They had seen
him make sick people well. 3Jesus went up a hill and he sat
down there with his disciples*. 4It was nearly the time for the
Jews'* Passover* Festival*.

5Jesus looked up. He saw a large crowd of people who were
coming towards him. Then he said to Philip, 'Where can we buy
enough bread to feed all these people?' 6Jesus himself already
knew what he would do. But he asked Philip this question for
a reason. He wanted to know what Philip would say. 7Philip
answered, 'A man might work for 8 months. But, he still would
not have enough money to buy bread for all these people. Still
there would not be enough bread for each person here to have
a little piece.' 8Then Andrew, another one of Jesus' disciples*,
spoke. He was Simon Peter's brother. He said to Jesus, 9'Here
is a boy who has 5 small loaves and two small fish. But
certainly, they will not be enough food for so many people.'

10Jesus said, 'Cause the people to sit down.' There was plenty
of grass in that place, so the people sat down. There were
about 5000 men. 11Jesus took the loaves and he thanked God
for them. Then he broke the loaves into pieces. He passed
them to all the people who were sitting there. Everyone had
all the bread that they wanted to eat. Jesus did the same with
the fish. 12When all the people had eaten enough food, Jesus
spoke. He said to his disciples*, 'Do not waste anything. Pick
up all the pieces that the people have not eaten.' 13So the
disciples* picked up all the pieces. They filled 12 baskets with
the pieces of bread that the people had not eaten.

14The people had seen this miracle* that Jesus had done. So,
they began to talk about it. They said, 'Certainly, this man
is the Prophet* who must come into the world.' 15The people
wanted to take Jesus so that they could make him their king.
But Jesus knew what they wanted to do. So, he went away
alone to the hills again.

Jesus walks on the water

16When it was evening, the disciples* went down to the lake.
17They got into a boat and they started to travel towards
Capernaum. It was dark then and Jesus still had not come to
them. 18A very strong wind was blowing and so the water was
moving powerfully. 19The disciples* were trying to pull the
boat through the water with oars (special long, flat pieces
of wood). When they had gone 3 or 4 miles (5-6 kilometres),
they saw Jesus. He was coming near to the boat and he was
walking on the water. And they were very afraid. 20But he
said to them, 'It is I. Do not be afraid.' 21So, the disciples*
were happy to let Jesus get into the boat with them.
Immediately, the boat came to the place where they wanted
to be.

The crowd looks for Jesus

22The crowd of people had stayed on the other side of the lake.
The next day, they looked round. They saw that the only boat
had gone. They knew that the disciples* had taken it. And they
knew that Jesus had not gone with his disciples*. 23(But other
boats from Tiberias had arrived near to the place where all
the people had eaten the bread. They had eaten that bread
after the LORD had thanked God for it.) 24The crowd saw that
neither Jesus nor his disciples* were there. So, they got into
the boats and they went to Capernaum. They were looking
for Jesus.

Jesus is the bread that causes us to live

25 The people found Jesus on the other side of the lake. So
they asked him, 'Teacher, when did you arrive here?' 26 Jesus
answered, 'I am telling you what is true. You saw me do
miracles*. But you are not looking for me because of that. No,
you are looking for me because you ate the loaves. You ate all
the bread that you wanted to eat. So then you were full. 27 Do
not work to get the food that does not continue. Instead, work
to get the food that does continue. Work to get the food that
causes you to live always. God, the Father, has put his mark of
authority upon the Son. That is why the Son of Man will give
this food to you.'

28 Then the people asked him, 'How can we do the work that
God wants us to do?' 29 Jesus answered, 'Believe him that God
has sent to you. That is the work that God wants you to do.'
30 So then the people asked him, 'What miracle* will you do? If
we see a miracle*, we will believe you. What will you do? 31 Our
ancestors* ate manna (special food from God) in the wild, dry
places*. As it says in the Old Testament*, "God gave bread to
them from heaven* so that they could eat it." ' 32 Jesus said
to them, 'I am telling you what is true. It was not Moses who
gave that bread to you from heaven*. No, but it is my Father
who really gives to you the bread from heaven*. 33 God's bread
is he who comes down from heaven*. He causes people in the
world to live.' 34 So they said to him, 'Sir, give this bread to us
now and always.'

35 Then Jesus said to them, 'I am the bread that causes people
to live. Anyone who comes to me will never be hungry. Anyone
who believes me will never be thirsty*. 36 But you have seen
me and still you do not believe me. I have told you that before.
37 Everyone that the Father gives to me will come to me. When
anyone comes to me, I will never send that person away.
38 I have not come down from heaven* to do what I myself
choose to do. No, instead I have come to obey him who sent me.
39 He who sent me does not want me to lose anyone. He does not

want me to lose even one of the people that he has given to me.
He wants me to raise all of them up on the last day, so that they
live with me always. 40These are the people who will be alive for
always: Everyone who sees the Son and believes him. And I will
raise them up on the last day. That is what my Father wants.'

41Jesus had said, 'I am the bread that came down from
heaven*.' When he said this, the Jews* did not like it. So, they
started to say bad things about Jesus. 42They said, 'But this is
Jesus, the son of Joseph. We know his father and his mother.
So, he should not say that he came down from heaven*.'

43Jesus answered, 'Stop saying these bad things to each other.
44The Father has sent me. Nobody can come to me unless the
Father brings them to me. And I will raise that person up on
the last day, so that they live with me always. 45The prophets*
wrote in the Old Testament*, "God will teach all the people."
These are the people who come to me: Everyone who hears
the Father and learns from him. 46I do not mean that anyone
has seen the Father. Nobody has seen the Father except
the Person who has come from God. It is he who has seen
the Father. 47I am telling you what is true. The person who
believes this is alive for always. 48I am the bread that causes
you to live. 49Your ancestors* ate the manna (special food from
God) in the wild, dry places*, but they died. 50This bread that
comes down from heaven* is different. Anyone who eats this
bread will not die. 51I am the bread that is alive. This bread
came down from heaven*. If anyone eats this bread, he will
live always. The bread that I will give is my body. I will give it
so that all people in the world can live.'

52Then the Jews* became angry and they quarrelled with each
other even more. They said, 'This man cannot give his body
to us so that we can eat it!' 53Jesus said to them, 'I tell you
what is true. You must eat the body of the Son of Man and
you must drink his blood. Unless you do those things, you are
not really alive. 54Every person needs to eat my body and they
need to drink my blood. If they do those things, they are alive
for always. And I will raise them up on the last day. 55My body

is proper food and my blood is proper drink. 56 Every person
needs to eat my body and they need to drink my blood. If a
person does that, that person lives in me. And I live in them.
57 The Father, who is alive, sent me. And I live because of him.
In the same way, anyone who eats me will live because of me.
58 This is the bread that came down from heaven*. It is not like
the manna (special food from God) that your ancestors* ate.
They ate it but they died. But the person who eats this bread
will live always.'

59 Jesus said these things while he was teaching in the
synagogue* at Capernaum.

Many disciples* go away from Jesus

60 Many of Jesus' disciples* did not like these words. They
said, 'This thing that he teaches is too difficult. Nobody can
agree with it!' 61 Jesus himself knew that the disciples* were
arguing. He did not need anyone to tell him. He said to them,
'This seems to make you surprised and angry. 62 So think
about this. The Son of Man goes up again to the place where
he was before. And you see him go up. Think about how you
would feel then. 63 It is the Spirit that causes you to live. The
body alone is worth nothing. The words that I have spoken
to you are spirit*. They cause you to live. 64 But some of you
do not believe.' Jesus had known from the beginning which
of them would not believe. Also, he had always known who
would sell him to his enemies*. 65 Then Jesus said these words:
'So I told you that only the Father can bring people to me.
Nobody can come to me unless the Father makes them able
to come.'

66 From that time, many of Jesus' disciples* left him. They did
not follow him any longer. 67 Then Jesus asked the 12 special
disciples*, 'Do you want to go away, too?' 68 Simon Peter
answered him, 'LORD, we do not know whom we would go
away to. You have the words that cause people to live always.
69 And we believe that you are the Holy One*. We believe that
you have come from God. We are sure about that.' 70 Jesus

replied, 'I have chosen the 12 of you. But one of you is a devil
(bad spirit* from Satan*)!' 71 He was speaking about Judas,
the son of Simon Iscariot. Judas was one of the 12 special
disciples*. But after this time he would sell Jesus to Jesus'
enemies*.

7

Jesus and his brothers

1 After this, Jesus visited many places in Galilee. He did not
want to visit Judea because the Jews'* leaders there wanted
to kill him. 2 It was almost time for the Jews'* Festival of
Tabernacles*. 3 So Jesus' brothers said to him, 'You should
leave this place and you should go to Judea. Then your
disciples* can see the great things that you do. 4 Nobody does
things secretly if he wants everyone to know him. You are
doing these things, so you should show yourself to everybody.'
5 Even his own brothers did not believe about him.

6 So Jesus answered, 'It is not the right time for me yet. But
any time is right for you. 7 People who belong to this world
cannot hate* you. But they hate* me. The things that they do
are wrong. And I show that those things are wrong. That is
why they hate* me. 8 You go to the festival*. I will not go to it
yet because it is not the right time for me yet.' 9 Jesus said this
and then he stayed in Galilee.

Jesus goes to the Festival of Tabernacles*

10 Some time after his brothers had gone, Jesus went to the
festival* also. But he did not let everybody know that he was
going. Instead, he went secretly. 11 The Jews'* leaders were
looking for him at the festival*. They asked, 'Where is that
man?' 12 Small groups in the crowd were talking quietly. Some
people said, 'He is a good man.' But other people said, 'No, he
is telling the people things that are not true.' 13 But nobody
spoke loudly about him, because they were afraid of the
Jews'* leaders.

14When about half of the time for the festival* had finished,
Jesus went to God's Great House (the temple). He started to
teach there. 15The Jews'* leaders were very surprised. They
asked, 'How does this man know so much? He has not learned
in our schools.' 16Jesus answered, 'What I teach does not
come from me. No, it comes from him who sent me. 17Anyone
can choose to do what God wants. Those people will know
about what I teach. They will know whether it comes from
God. And they will know if it comes from my own thoughts.
18A person who teaches his own ideas wants people to think
great things about him. But a person who wants to show
great things about someone else is different. A person like
that wants people to think great things about him who sent
him. A person like that is honest and there is nothing false in
him. 19Moses gave God's rules to you. But not one of you obeys
those rules. Why are you trying to kill me?'

20The crowd answered, 'You have a demon (bad spirit* from
Satan*). Who is trying to kill you?' 21Jesus replied, 'I have
done one miracle* on the Sabbath* day, and all of you were
surprised. 22 But you will circumcise* a boy on the Sabbath*
day. Moses told you that you must circumcise* your sons. That
is why you will do it. Your ancestors* did it even before Moses
was born. 23You will circumcise* a boy on the Sabbath* day so
that you obey Moses' rules. So you should not be angry with
me because I made a man completely well on the Sabbath*
day. 24Do not judge* about things because of what they may
seem to be. Instead, judge* about things because of what
is right.'

The people talk about whether Jesus is the Messiah*

25Some of the people in Jerusalem began to say, 'This is the
man that the leaders want to kill. 26But look! He is speaking
to the crowds. And the leaders are not saying anything to
him! Perhaps they think that he is really the Christ*! 27But we
know where this man came from. When the Christ* comes,

nobody will know that. Nobody will know where he has
come from.'

28 Jesus was teaching in God's Great House (the temple). He
shouted, 'Yes, you know me. And you know where I came
from. I have not come because I myself decided to come. He
who sent me is true. You do not know him. 29 But I know him
because I have come from him. He sent me.' 30 When they
heard this, they tried to take him to a prison. But nobody
put their hands on him, because it was not the right time. It
was not the right time for that to happen. 31 But many people
in the crowd believed him. They said, 'This man has done so
many miracles*. Nobody could do more miracles*. Surely he is
the Christ*!'

32 The Pharisees* heard what the crowds were saying quietly
about Jesus. Then the most important priests* and the
Pharisees* sent some soldiers to take him away. 33 Jesus
said, 'I will be with you for only a short time. Then I will go to
him who sent me. 34 You will look for me, but you will not find
me. You cannot go to the place where I will be.' 35 The Jews'*
leaders asked each other, 'What is he trying to tell us? Where
can he go so that we cannot find him? Perhaps he will go to
our people who live among the Greeks*. Perhaps he will go to
teach the Greeks. 36 He says, "You will look for me, but you will
not find me." And he says, "You cannot go to the place where
I will be." What does he mean?'

Streams of the water that causes people to live

37 The last day of the festival* was the most important day.
On that day, Jesus stood up and he spoke with a loud voice.
He said, 'If anyone is thirsty*, he should come to me. He
should come to me and he should drink. 38 As it says in the
Old Testament*, "God will cause streams of water to pour
out from anyone who believes me. Streams of the water that
causes people to live will come out from inside that person." '
39 Jesus was speaking about God's Spirit, who would come
to people some time after that. Those people who believed

Jesus would receive God's Spirit then. But God had not given
his Spirit yet, because he had not raised Jesus yet. He had
not yet raised Jesus, so that Jesus could be in heaven* with
him again.

The people argue

40 Some of the people in the crowd heard Jesus say these
words. Then they said, 'This man really is the Prophet* that
we were waiting for!' 41 Other people said, 'This man is the
Christ*.' But some people said, 'The Prophet* will not come
from Galilee! 42 The Old Testament* says that the Christ* will
come from King David's family*. He will come from Bethlehem,
the town where David lived.' 43 So, the crowd of people could
not agree about Jesus. 44 Some people wanted to take him to a
prison. But nobody put their hands on him to take him away.

45 The soldiers returned to the most important priests* and
the Pharisees*. They asked the soldiers, 'Why did you not
bring him here?' 46 The soldiers answered, 'Nobody has ever
spoken like this man speaks.' 47 The Pharisees* replied, 'He
seems to have caused you to believe these silly things! 48 None
of the Pharisees* or the leaders believes him. Surely, you know
that! 49 But this crowd does not know Moses' rules. So, God
will cause very bad things to happen to them.' 50 Nicodemus
was one of the Pharisees*. He was the man who had gone to
see Jesus before. He said to the other people, 51 'Our rules say
that we must listen to a man first. We must find out first what
he has done. Only then can we judge* him.' 52 They answered,
'Perhaps you come from Galilee, too! Study the Scriptures (Old
Testament*). You will learn from them that no prophet* ever
comes from Galilee.' 53 Then everyone went to his own home.

8

The woman who was with a man who was not her husband

[1] But Jesus went to the Mount (mountain) of Olives*. [2]Early the
next morning, he returned to God's Great House (the temple).
All the people came to him. He sat down and he began to
teach them.

[3]The Pharisees* and the scribes (men who taught God's rules)
brought a woman to him. They had found her with another
man. She was having sex with a man who was not her husband.
They caused her to stand in front of all the people there. [4]They
said to Jesus, 'Teacher, we found this woman. She was having
sex with a man who was not her husband. [5]Moses' rules say
that we should throw stones at this kind of woman, to kill her.
What do you say about this?' [6]They asked this question for a
reason. They wanted Jesus to say something that they could
use against him. But Jesus bent himself down. He started to
write on the ground with his finger.

[7]They continued to ask him questions. Then he stood up. He
said to them, 'If any one of you has never done anything
wrong, he can throw the first stone at her.' [8]He bent himself
down again and he wrote on the ground. [9]When they heard
this, they began to leave. They went one at a time. The older
ones went first. So then Jesus was alone with the woman.
She was still standing there. [10]Jesus stood up. He said to her,
'Woman, where are they? There seems to be nobody still here
who wants to punish* you.' [11]She said, 'There is nobody, Sir.'
So Jesus said, 'And I do not want to punish* you. Go away and
do not do wrong things again.'

Jesus is the light of the world

[12]Jesus spoke to the people again. He said, 'I am the light of
the world. Anyone who becomes my disciple* will never walk in

the dark. No, he will have the light that causes people to live.'
13 The Pharisees* began to argue with him. They said, 'You are
saying things about yourself. But you are only one man. So,
what you say is not certainly true.'

14 Jesus answered, 'What I say is true. Even if I do speak on
my own behalf, my words are true. I know where I came
from. I know where I will go. But you do not know where
I came from. You do not know where I will go. 15 You judge*
in a human way. I do not judge* anyone. 16 But if I did judge*
anyone, I would judge* correctly. That is because I am not
alone. The Father, who sent me, is with me. 17 Your rules say,
"There must be two people who agree about something. If
there are two people, their words are true." 18 I speak on my
own behalf. The Father, who sent me, speaks about me also.'

19 Then they asked him, 'Where is your Father?' Jesus
answered, 'You do not know either me or my Father. If you
knew me, you would know my Father also.' 20 Jesus said all
these words while he taught in God's Great House (the temple).
He was near the place where they kept the gifts of money.
Nobody took him away to a prison, because it was not the
right time for that yet.

Jesus says that he comes from above

21 Jesus said to them again, 'I will go away and you will look
for me. But you are sinful* and you will die sinful*. You cannot
go where I will go.' 22 So, the Jews'* leaders said to each other,
'Perhaps he means that he will kill himself. He says, "You
cannot go where I will go." Perhaps that is why he says this.'
23 Jesus answered, 'You belong to the things down here. But
I come from above. You belong to this world, but I do not
belong to this world. 24 That is why I told you this. I told you
that you would die sinful*. You must believe that "I am". If you
will not believe, you will die sinful*.'

25 Then they asked him, 'Who are you?' Jesus answered, 'I have
told you who I am from the beginning. That is who I am.

26 I have many things to say about you. I must judge* about
many things that you do. But he who sent me is true. I tell
the world only what I have heard from him.' 27 They did not
understand that he was speaking to them about the Father.
28 So Jesus said, 'You will lift up the Son of Man. Then you
will know that "I am". And you will know that I do nothing by
myself. I say only what the Father has taught me to say. 29 He
who sent me is with me. He has not caused me to be alone,
because I obey him always. I do always the things that he
wants me to do.' 30 Many people who heard Jesus say these
things believed him.

What is true will make you free

31 Then Jesus spoke to the Jews* who believed him. He said,
'Continue to obey the words that I have spoken to you. If you
continue to do that, you are really my disciples*. 32 And you
will know what is true. And what is true will make you free.'
33 They answered him, 'We are Abraham's grandchildren. We
have never been anyone's slaves. But you say to us, "You will
become free." What do you mean?'

34 Jesus answered them, 'I am telling you what is true.
Everyone who does sinful* things is a slave to sin*. 35 A slave
does not belong to a family for always. But a son does belong
to a family for always. 36 So, if the Son makes you free, you will
really be free. 37 I know that you are Abraham's grandchildren.
But you are trying to kill me, because you have no room in
yourselves for my words. 38 I speak about what my Father has
shown me. But you do what you have heard from your father.'

39 They answered, 'Abraham is our father!' Jesus replied, 'If
you were really Abraham's children, you would be like him. You
would do the same things that he did. 40 I am a man who has
told you only true things. I have told you the true things that
I have heard from God. But you want to kill me. Abraham did
not do anything like that! 41 You do the same things that your
father does.' They said to him, 'God himself is our only Father,
and we are his proper sons!'

[42] Jesus said to them, 'If God was really your Father, you would
love me. I came from God and now I am here. I did not come
because it was my own idea. No, but God sent me. [43] Why do
you not understand what I say? It is because you cannot
really hear my message. [44] You are the children of your father,
the Devil*. And you want to do the things that he wants. From
the beginning, he was someone who killed people. He did not
continue with what is true. There is nothing true in him. He
says things that are not true. And then he is showing what
he himself is like. He is the father of everything that is not
true. [45] But I tell you what is true. And that is why you do not
believe me. [46] None of you can show that I have done anything
wrong. You should believe me, because I am telling you true
things. [47] Someone who is God's hears God's words. But you are
not God's. That is why you do not hear.'

[48] The Jews* answered him, 'What we say about you is right!
You are from Samaria and you have a demon (bad spirit* from
Satan*) in you!' [49] Jesus replied, 'There is no demon in me.' 'But
I want people to know how great and how good my Father is.
And you want people to think bad things about me. [50] I myself
am not wanting people to think great things about me. There
is someone who does want people to think great things about
me. And it is he who judges* correctly about me. [51] I am telling
you what is true. If anyone obeys my words, he will never die.'
[52] The Jews* shouted, 'Now we know that a demon (bad spirit*)
lives in you! Abraham and all the prophets* died. But you say,
"Anyone who obeys my words will never die!" [53] You cannot be
greater than our father Abraham, who died! You cannot be
greater than all the prophets*, who died! Who do you think
that you are?'

[54] Jesus replied, 'If I myself wanted people to think great
things about me, that would be worth nothing. But it is my
Father who wants that. And you say that he is your God. [55] You
have never known him, but I know him. I might say, "I do not
know him." But then I would be saying something that is not
true. So, I would be like you. But I do know him, and I obey

his words. 56 Your father Abraham knew that I would come. He
knew that he would see that time. He knew that he would be
very happy then. He did see that time, and he was very happy.'

57 The Jews* said, 'You are not 50 years old yet. But you say
that you have seen Abraham!' 58 Jesus said, 'I am telling you
what is true. Before Abraham was even born, "I am".' 59 Then
they picked up stones so that they could throw them at him.
But Jesus hid himself, and he went out of God's Great House
(the temple).

9

Jesus makes a man able to see

1 While Jesus was walking along, he saw a certain man. This
man had been unable to see since he was born. 2 Jesus'
disciples* asked him, 'Teacher, why was this man born
unable to see? Was it because he himself did something
wrong? Or was it because his parents did something wrong?'
3 Jesus answered, 'It was not because either this man or
his parents did something wrong. It happened so that God
could show his work in this man. 4 While it is still day, we
must continue to work. We must do the work of him who
sent me. We must work now because it will be night soon.
Then nobody can work. 5 While I am in the world, I am the
world's light.'

6 When Jesus had finished speaking, he spat (sent water from
his mouth) on the ground. He mixed it on the ground so that
he made mud*. Then he put some of the mud* on the eyes of
the man who was unable to see. 7 Jesus said to him, 'Go and
wash in the Siloam pool.' (The name Siloam means 'sent'.) So
the man went there and he washed himself. When he returned,
he could see.

8 Then people who knew the man began to talk about him. Also,
people who had seen him before spoke to each other about
him. They had seen him when he was asking for money. They

asked, 'Is this the man who sat here? Is this the man who
asked for money?' 9 Some people said, 'Yes, it is him.' But other
people said, 'No, it is someone who is very like him.' So the
man himself said, 'I am that man.' 10 Then they asked him, 'How
did you become able to see?' 11 He answered, 'The man called
Jesus made some mud*. He put the mud* on my eyes. Then
he sent me to wash in the Siloam pool. So I went there and
I washed. And then I could see.' 12 They asked him, 'Where is
this man?' He replied, 'I do not know.'

The Pharisees* talk to the man who had been unable to see

13 The people brought the man who had been unable to see to
the Pharisees*. 14 (Jesus had made the mud* and then he had
caused the man to see on a Sabbath* day.) 15 So the Pharisees*
asked the man again, 'How did you become able to see?' The
man replied, 'Jesus put mud* on my eyes. Then I washed and
now I can see.'

16 So some of the Pharisees* said, 'This man (Jesus) cannot
have come from God. He does not obey the rules about the
Sabbath* day.' But other Pharisees* said, 'Nobody who is
sinful* could do great things like this!' So they did not agree
with each other. 17 The Pharisees* spoke again to the man who
had been unable to see. They said, 'What do you yourself
say about this man who has made you able to see?' The man
replied, 'He is a prophet*.'

18 The Jews'* leaders did not want to believe that the man
had really been unable to see. They did not want to believe
that he had become able to see. So, they sent people to ask
the man's parents to come to them. 19 They asked the parents,
'Is this your son? You say, "When he was born, he was unable
to see." But now he can see. How did this happen?' 20 The
parents replied, 'We know that this is our son. And when he
was born, he was unable to see. We know that, too. 21 But
we do not know how he can see now. And we do not know
who made him able to see. Ask him. He is old enough. He

himself can answer!' 22The man's parents said these things
because they were afraid of the Jews'* leaders. The Jews'*
leaders did not want anyone to say that Jesus was the
Christ*. They had already agreed to punish* anyone who said
that. The leaders would not let anyone like that belong to the
synagogue*. 23That is why the man's parents said, 'Ask him.
He is old enough.'

24So the leaders asked again to speak to the man who had
been unable to see. They said to him, 'Promise that you will
speak only true things. Promise that in front of God. We know
that this man is sinful*.' 25The man replied, 'I do not know
whether he is sinful* or not. But I do know one thing. I was
unable to see and now I can see. I do know that.' 26Then they
asked him, 'What did he do to you? How did he make you able
to see?' 27He answered them, 'I have told you already and you
would not listen. Why do you want to hear it again? Do you
want to become his disciples* too?' 28Then they were very
angry with him. They shouted at him, 'You are that man's
disciple*. But we are Moses' disciples*. 29We know that God
spoke to Moses. But we do not even know where this man
comes from.'

30The man answered, 'That is a very strange thing! You do not
know where Jesus comes from. But it was he who made me able
to see. 31We know that God does not listen to sinful* people.
But God does listen to some people:

People who believe how great he is.

People who do what he wants them to do.

He does listen to those people. We know that. 32Nobody before
has ever made a man able to see, who was born unable to see.
Since the world began, nobody has ever done that! 33Surely, this
man who made me able to see has come from God. Unless he
came from God, he could not do anything.' 34The Jews'* leaders
answered, 'You have always been sinful*, since the day that you
were born. You cannot try to teach us!' And they threw him out.

Jesus came to cause people really to see

35 Jesus heard that the Jews'* leaders had thrown the man out.
So, he found the man. And Jesus asked him, 'Do you believe
the Son of Man?' 36 The man answered, 'Sir, please tell me who
he is. Then I can believe him.' 37 Jesus said to him, 'You have
seen him. It is he who is talking to you now. I am he.' 38 Then
the man said, 'LORD, I believe.' He bent down on his knees and
he worshipped* Jesus.

39 Then Jesus said, 'I came into this world to show what people
are really like. So then, those people who do not see will be able
to see. And those people who do see will become unable to see.'
40 Some of the Pharisees* who were there with him heard this.
They asked Jesus, 'Do you mean that we are unable to see also?'
41 Jesus said to them, 'If you were unable to see, you would not
have done anything wrong. But you say that you can see. So,
that means that you are still continuing to do something wrong.'

10

The story about the shepherd*

1 Jesus said, 'I am telling you what is true. A shepherd* keeps
his sheep in a safe place with a wall round it. There is a gate
into that safe place. Anyone else who gets into that place
by another way, not through the gate, is not the shepherd*.
That person is bad. He comes to take away the sheep that
are not his. 2 The shepherd* goes in through the gate. 3 The
person who watches the gate opens it for the shepherd*. The
sheep recognise the shepherd's* voice. He calls each of his
own sheep by their name and he leads them out. 4 When he
has brought all his own sheep out, he goes in front of them.
And the sheep follow him because they know his voice. 5 They
will not follow a stranger. They will run away from a stranger
because they do not recognise his voice.'

6 Jesus told them this story that was like a picture. But they
did not understand what he was saying to them.

Jesus is like the good shepherd*

7 So Jesus spoke again. 'I am telling you what is true. I am
like the gate for the sheep*. 8 All other men who ever came to
the sheep* before me were bad. They wanted to take away
the sheep that were not theirs. But the sheep did not listen
to them. 9 I am like the gate. Anyone who comes in through
me will be safe. He will come in and he will go out. And he will
find plenty of food. 10 He who comes to take away my sheep*
comes only to kill them. He comes only to destroy. I have come
so that they can live. And so they can have everything that
they need.'

11 'I am like the good shepherd*. The good shepherd* would die
so that he can save his sheep. 12 Another man may work with
the sheep so that he gets money. But the sheep are not his
own. A man like that is not the shepherd*. A man like that runs
away when he sees a wolf (a wild dog). The wolf comes to kill
the sheep. But a man like that leaves the sheep and he runs
away. So, the wolf attacks the sheep and it causes them to run
in all directions. 13 That man runs away because the sheep are
not his own. The sheep do not really matter to him.'

14 'I am like the good shepherd*. I know my own sheep*, and
they know me. 15 I know them in the same way that my Father
knows me. And they know me in the same way that I know the
Father. And I will die on behalf of the sheep*. 16 I have other
sheep* also, and I must bring them too. They do not belong to
this group of sheep. But they will listen to my voice, and so all
the sheep will become one group, with one shepherd*. 17 The
Father loves me because I will choose to die. I will choose to
die so that then I can become alive again. 18 Nobody causes me
to die. No, instead, I myself choose to die. I have authority so
that I can choose to die. Also, I have authority so that I can
become alive again. My Father has said that I must do that.'

[19]Again, the Jews* could not agree about these things that
Jesus said. [20]Many of them said, 'He has a demon (bad spirit*
from Satan*) and he is crazy. You should not listen to him!'
[21]But other people said, 'A man with a demon (bad spirit*)
could not talk like this! A demon could not make people able
to see!'

The Jews'* leaders do not believe Jesus

[22]It was the time for the Dedication* Festival* at Jerusalem.

[23]It was winter. And Jesus was walking under a roof by
the side of God's Great House (the temple). The place was
called Solomon's porch*. [24]The Jews'* leaders stood round
him. They said to him, 'We want to be sure about who you
are. When will you tell us? If you are the Christ*, tell us
clearly.' [25]Jesus answered, 'I have told you, but you do not
believe. The things that I do by my Father's authority show
you about me. Those things show you who I am. [26]But you
refuse to believe, because you do not belong to my sheep*.
[27]My sheep* recognise my voice. I know them, and they follow
me. [28]I cause them to live always. They will never die. Nobody
can ever take them away from me. [29]My Father, who has given
them to me, is greater than all things. Nobody can ever take
my sheep* out of my Father's hand. [30]My Father and I are
one Person.'

[31]Then the Jews'* leaders picked up stones again to throw at
Jesus so that they could kill him. [32]Jesus said to them, 'I have
done many good things. The Father told me that I must do
them. You have seen me do those good things. Which of those
good things have caused you to throw stones at me?' [33]The
Jews'* leaders answered, 'We do not want to kill you with
stones because of any good things that you have done. We
want to kill you with stones because you are speaking against
God. You are only a man. But you are saying that you are God.'

[34]Jesus answered, 'It says in your own Scriptures (Old
Testament*) that God said, "You are gods." [35]God called

the people to whom he spoke 'gods'. And the Scriptures are
always true. 36The Father chose me. And he sent me into
the world. I said that I am God's Son. So you should not say,
because of that, that I speak against God. 37If I am not doing
my Father's work, do not believe me. 38But if I am doing his
work, believe that work. Even if you do not believe me, believe
my work. Believe the things that I do. Then you will know
certainly that the Father is in me. And you will know that I am
in the Father.'

39Again, the Jews'* leaders tried to catch Jesus. But he got
away from them.

40Jesus returned across the Jordan river again. He went to
the place where John had baptised* people. And Jesus stayed
there. 41Many people came to him. They said to each other,
'John did not do any miracles*. But everything that John said
about this man was true.' 42And in that place, many people
believed Jesus.

11

Lazarus dies

1A certain man, who was called Lazarus, became ill. Lazarus
lived at Bethany, the village where Mary and her sister
Martha lived too. 2It was this Mary who had poured oil with a
lovely smell over the LORD. Then she had cleaned his feet with
her hair. It was her brother Lazarus who was ill. 3So the two
sisters sent a message to Jesus. The message said, 'LORD, the
friend that you love is ill.'

4Jesus heard the message. Then he said, 'This illness will
not finish with Lazarus's death. No, its purpose is to show
how great and how powerful God is. It will show how great
God's Son is.' 5Jesus loved Martha and her sister, and their
brother Lazarus, too. 6He heard the news that Lazarus was
ill. But then he stayed in the place where he was for two
more days.

7After that, Jesus said to his disciples*, 'We will return to
Judea.' 8The disciples* said, 'Teacher, only a short time ago,
the Jews* there tried to kill you with stones. You should not
return there!' 9Jesus answered, 'You know that there are 12
hours in the day. Anyone who walks during the day will not fall
down. He will not fall down because he sees this world's light.
10But anyone who walks during the night will fall down. He will
fall down because there is no light in him.'

11Jesus said that. Then he said to them, 'Our friend Lazarus
is sleeping. But I go there to wake him up.' 12So the disciples*
said to him, 'If he is sleeping, LORD, he will get well.' 13But Jesus
meant that Lazarus had died. The disciples* thought that
Jesus was talking about sleep as rest. 14So then, Jesus told
them clearly, 'Lazarus is dead. 15But I am happy that I was not
with him. I am happy about that because now you will believe.
We must go to him now.' 16Thomas, who was called Didymus*,
spoke to the other disciples*. He said, 'We will go with our
Teacher, so that we can die with him!'

Jesus is able to make dead people alive

17Jesus arrived at Bethany. Then he discovered that they
had buried Lazarus 4 days earlier. 18Bethany was less than 2
miles (about 3 kilometres) from Jerusalem. 19Many Jews* had
come there to visit Martha and Mary. These Jews* wanted
to be kind to Martha and Mary because their brother
had died.

20Martha heard the news that Jesus was coming. So
immediately, she went out to meet him. But Mary stayed at
home. 21Martha said to Jesus, 'LORD, if you had been here,
my brother would not have died. 22But I know that, even
now, God will answer you. God will do whatever you ask
him.' 23Jesus told her, 'Your brother will rise, to become alive
again.' 24Martha replied, 'I know that he will rise, to become
alive again, on the last day.' 25Jesus said to her, 'It is I who
raise dead people, to make them alive. I cause people to
live. Anyone who believes me will live. Even if that person

dies, he will live. 26 Some people will live and believe in me.
Anyone who does that will never die. Do you believe that?'
27 She answered, 'Yes, LORD, I believe that you are the Christ*,
God's Son. You are the man that God promised to send into
the world.'

Jesus weeps

28 After this, Martha went home and she spoke secretly to
her sister, Mary. Martha said, 'The Teacher is here, and he
is asking to meet you.' 29 When Mary heard this, she got up.
She hurried out to meet Jesus. 30 Jesus had not arrived in
the village yet. He was still in the place where Martha had
met him. 31 The Jews* in the house, who were being kind to
Mary, saw her get up quickly. They saw her go out and so they
followed her. They thought that she was going to the tomb* to
weep there.

32 Mary arrived at the place where Jesus was. When she saw
Jesus, she fell at his feet. She said, 'LORD, if you had been here,
my brother would not have died.' 33 Jesus saw that Mary was
weeping. The Jews* who had come with her were weeping, too.
Jesus saw them and he felt very, very sad in his spirit*. He was
very sorry for them. 34 He asked them, 'Where have you put
his dead body?' They answered, 'Come and see, LORD.' 35 Jesus
wept. 36 Then the Jews* said to each other, 'See how much he
loved Lazarus!' 37 But some of them said, 'He opened the eyes
of the man who could not see. So, surely he would have been
able to stop Lazarus from dying.'

Jesus makes Lazarus alive again

38 Jesus felt very, very sad again while he was coming to the
tomb*. It was a big hole in the rock. A very big stone covered
the way into it. 39 Jesus said, 'Take the stone away.' Martha,
the dead man's sister, said to Jesus, 'But LORD, his dead body
will have a bad smell. He has been dead for 4 days!' 40 Jesus
said to her, 'I told you that you must believe. Then, as a result,
you will see how great and how powerful God is. That is what

I told you.' 41 So they took the stone away. Jesus looked up
towards the sky. He said, 'Father, I thank you that you have
listened to me. 42 I know that you listen to me always. But
I said this because of all the people who are standing here.
I want them to believe that you sent me.' 43 When Jesus had
said this, he shouted with a loud voice, 'Lazarus, come out!'
44 The dead man came out. There were pieces of cloth round
his hands and round his feet. Another piece of cloth was round
his face. Jesus said to them, 'Undo the cloths and let him go.'

The Pharisees* decide how to kill Jesus

45 Many of the Jews* who had come to visit Mary saw this.
They saw what Jesus did. So, they believed him. 46 But some of
them went to the Pharisees*. They told the Pharisees* what
Jesus had done. 47 Then the Pharisees* and the most important
priests* had a meeting. They said to each other, 'What will
we do? This man is doing so many miracles*. 48 If we let him
do more things like this, everyone will believe him. Then the
Romans* will come. And they will destroy our temple (God's
Great House) and they will kill our people.'

49 One of them, who was called Caiaphas, was the priests'*
leader that year. He said, 'You do not understand the problem.
50 It is better that one man should die on behalf of the people.
That is better than if all the people in our country died.'
51 Caiaphas did not say this because he had thought it by
himself. No, he was speaking as a prophet* because he was
the priests'* leader that year. He spoke as a prophet* that
Jesus would die on behalf of Israel's people. 52 And Jesus would
die not only for Israel's people. Also, his death would bring
together all God's people who lived in many different places.
They would become like one big family*.

53 From that day, the Jews'* leaders decided together how they
could kill Jesus. 54 So, Jesus stopped travelling about in Judea
where everyone could see him. Instead, he went away secretly
to a town called Ephraim. It was near to the wild place*. He
stayed there with the disciples*.

55 It was almost time for the Jews'* Passover* Festival*. Many
people were going from their country places to Jerusalem.
They were going to make themselves clean and ready for God
before they went to the festival*. 56 They were looking for
Jesus. While they were standing in God's Great House (the
temple), they spoke to each other about him. They asked each
other, 'Do you think that he will come to the festival* or not?'
57 The most important priests* and the Pharisees* had spoken
to the people about Jesus. They had told them, 'Someone may
know where Jesus is. If anyone does know that, you must tell
us.' So then they could put him in a prison.

12

Jesus at Bethany

1 Six days before the Passover*, Jesus went to Bethany, the
village where Lazarus lived. He was the man who had been
dead. But Jesus had raised him, to make him alive again.
2 Some friends prepared a special meal there for Jesus. Martha
gave out the food, and Lazarus sat among the visitors, with
Jesus. 3 Then Mary brought a pound of very expensive oil that
had a lovely smell. She poured it over Jesus' feet and then she
cleaned his feet with her hair. The smell of the oil filled the
whole house.

4 Then Judas Iscariot, one of Jesus' disciples*, spoke. He
was the man who would sell Jesus to Jesus' enemies*. Judas
said, 5 'She could have sold this expensive oil for as much
money as someone would get for a year's work. And she could
have given that money to poor people.' 6 He did not say this
because he really wanted to help the poor people. No, he said
it because he wanted the money himself. He kept the bag of
money, and sometimes he took money from it for himself. 7 But
Jesus said, 'Do not stop her! She has kept this oil for the day
when they bury my dead body. 8 Poor people will always be
with you, but I will not always be with you.'

9 By this time, a large crowd of Jews* had heard the news that
Jesus was at Bethany. So, they came there to see him. They
came also to see Lazarus, because Jesus had made him alive
again. 10 So the most important priests*, who had already
decided to kill Jesus, decided to kill Lazarus too. 11 They
decided to do that because many Jews* were refusing to obey
them. Instead, these Jews* were believing Jesus because of
what he had done for Lazarus.

Jesus goes into Jerusalem as the Messiah*

12 The next day, a large crowd of people were in Jerusalem
for the festival*. They heard the news that Jesus was on the
way there. 13 So, they took branches from palm* trees and
they went out to meet Jesus. They were shouting, 'Save us
now! God is good to the man who comes in the name of the
LORD. God is good to the King of Israel!' 14 Jesus found a young
donkey*. And he sat on it, as it says in the Old Testament*:

15 'Do not be afraid, people in Zion (Jerusalem).

> Look! Your king is coming.
>
> He is riding on a young donkey*.'

16 Jesus' disciples* did not understand all this at that time.
They understood only after Jesus had returned to God in
heaven*. Then they remembered that the Old Testament* said
these things about him. And they remembered that these
things had happened to him. 17 The crowd who had been with
Jesus before, continued to tell people about Lazarus. Jesus
had told Lazarus that he should come out of the tomb*. Jesus
had made Lazarus alive again after he had been dead. The
crowd continued to tell people about this. 18 That is why all the
people came to meet Jesus. They had heard that he had done
this miracle*. 19 So, the Pharisees* said to each other, 'This
is not what we wanted. Look! All the people in the world are
running after him!'

Jesus says that he will soon die

20There were some Greeks (people from Greece) among the
people who had come to worship* God at the festival*. 21These
Greeks came to Philip, who was from Bethsaida city in Galilee.
They said to him, 'Sir, we want to talk with Jesus.' 22Philip went
to Andrew and he told Andrew this. Then Philip and Andrew
went to Jesus and they told him.

23Jesus said to them, 'God will show how great and how good
the Son of Man is. It is now time for that to happen. 24I am
telling you what is true. A seed of wheat* continues to be only
a single seed unless it dies. It must fall into the ground and
then it must die. But if it dies, it grows to give a lot of seeds.'

25'Anyone who loves his own life will lose it. But anyone who
hates* his life in this world will live always. 26Anyone who
wants to be my servant must follow me. Then he will be with
me, where I am. My Father will do great things for anyone
who is my servant. 27Now I feel very sad. And I have trouble in
my mind. I might say, "Father, save me from this very difficult
time!" But I came to the world for this purpose. I came so that
I could go through this difficult time. 28Father, show how great
and how good you are.'

Then someone spoke from heaven*, 'I have shown how great
and how good I am. And I will do it again.' 29The crowd of
people who were standing there heard the sound of this voice.
And they said that it was like the noise of a storm. But other
people said, 'An angel* spoke to him!'

30Jesus said, 'This voice did not speak so that it could help
me. No, it spoke so that it could help you. 31It is time now for
God to judge* the people in this world. Now he will throw out
the ruler of this world. 32But when people lift me up from the
earth, then I will pull everyone towards myself.' 33He said this
to show how he would soon die.

34The crowd said, 'The Scriptures (Old Testament*) tell us that
the Christ* will continue always. So why do you say, "People
must lift up the Son of Man"? Who is this Son of Man?' 35Jesus
answered, 'The light will be with you for only a short time
longer. So, continue to walk while you still have the light. Then
the dark will not come over you. Anyone who walks in the dark
does not know the way. That person does not know where he
is going. 36Believe the light, while you have the light. So then
you will become sons of light.' When Jesus had said this, he
went away. And he hid himself from them.

The Jews* still do not believe Jesus

37Jesus had done so many miracles* that the people
themselves had seen. But even then, they still did not believe
him. 38This showed that the prophet* Isaiah had spoken true
words. Isaiah had said:

'LORD, nobody has believed our message.

Nobody has understood how powerful the LORD is.'

39Isaiah spoke also about why the people could not believe.
40He said:

'God has made their eyes unable to see.

He has closed their minds.

So they cannot see with their eyes, and they cannot understand with their minds.

They will not turn to me, so that I can make them well.'

41Isaiah had seen how great Christ is. That is why he said
these things.

42But many of the Jews'* leaders did believe Jesus. But they
did not tell people that they believed. They did not speak
about it because they were afraid of the Pharisees*. They were
afraid that the Pharisees* would send them away from the

synagogue*. 43They wanted other people to think good things
about them more than they wanted to make God happy.

Jesus' words will judge* people

44Jesus said in a loud voice, 'Anyone who believes me does not
believe only me. That person believes also him who sent me.
45Anyone who looks at me does not see only me. That person
sees also him who sent me. 46I have come into the world to be
a light. Everyone who believes me will not remain in the dark.
That is why I came. 47Some people may hear my words but
not obey them. I will not judge* anyone who does that. I did
not come to judge* the people in the world. I came to save
them. 48Something else will judge* anyone who refuses me.
Something else will judge* anyone who will not listen to my
words. The message that I have spoken will judge* him on the
last day. 49The words that I have spoken did not come from me
myself. They came from the Father, who sent me. He told me
what to say. And he told me how to say it. 50What the Father
says causes people to live always. I know that. So, I say only
those things that the Father has said to me.'

13

Jesus washes his disciples'* feet

1It was nearly time for the Passover* Festival*. Jesus knew
that it was almost time for him to leave this world. It was
almost time for him to go to the Father. He had always loved
those people in the world who were his own. And he loved
them to the end.

2Jesus and his disciples* were eating supper. The Devil* had
already put an idea into the mind of Judas Iscariot, Simon's
son. The idea was to sell Jesus to his enemies*. 3Jesus knew
that the Father had given him power* over everything. He
knew that he had come from God. And he knew that he would
soon return to God. 4So, during the meal, he stood up. He took
off the coat that he wore over his other clothes. He tied a

thick cloth round his body. 5Then he poured water into a bowl
(a wide pot) and he began to wash the disciples'* feet. Jesus
made their feet dry with the thick cloth that was round him.

6Jesus came to Simon Peter. Peter asked him, 'LORD, will you
wash my feet?' 7Jesus answered him, 'You do not understand
now what I am doing. But you will understand some time
after this.' 8Peter said, 'You will never, never wash my feet!'
Jesus answered, 'If I do not wash you, you do not belong with
me.' 9Simon Peter replied, 'So LORD, do not wash my feet only!
Wash my hands and my head too!' 10Jesus said, 'A person who
has had a bath is completely clean. He needs only to wash his
feet. And all of you are clean, except one of you.' 11Jesus knew
already who would sell him to his enemies*. That is why he
said, 'All of you are clean, except one.'

12When he had finished washing their feet, Jesus put on his
coat. He returned to his place at the meal. He asked them,
'I want you to understand what I have just done to you. 13You
call me Teacher and LORD. And you are right when you say that.
You are right, because I am your Teacher and LORD. 14I am
your Teacher and your LORD, and I have washed your feet. So,
you should wash each other's feet also. 15I have given you an
example. So, you should do the same as I have done for you.
16I am telling you what is true. No slave is more important
than his master is. And no messenger* is more important than
the person who sent him. 17Now you know these things. So,
you will be happy if you do them.'

18'I am not talking about all of you. I know the people that
I have chosen. The Old Testament* says, "Someone who ate
food with me has become my enemy*." So that is what must
happen. 19I am telling you this now, before it happens. So then,
when it does happen, you will believe. You will believe that
"I am". 20I am telling you what is true. Some people will accept
those that I send. And anyone who accepts them is accepting
me also. And so some people will accept me. And anyone like
that is accepting also him who sent me.'

Jesus tells the disciples* that one of them will sell him to his enemies*

21 After Jesus had said this, he felt very, very sad. And he
had trouble in his mind. He said to them very seriously, 'I am
telling you what is true. One of you will sell me to my enemies*.'
22 The disciples* looked at each other. They did not know which
of them Jesus was speaking about. 23 One of them, the disciple*
that Jesus loved, was sitting very near to Jesus. 24 Simon Peter
pointed at that disciple*. Peter said, 'Ask Jesus whom he is
speaking about.' 25 So that disciple* moved even nearer to
Jesus and he asked, 'Who is it, LORD?' 26 Jesus answered, 'I will
put a piece of bread in the dish of food. Then I will give the
bread to him. That is the man.' So he put a piece of bread in
the dish. Then he gave it to Judas, the son of Simon Iscariot.

27 Then, when Judas had taken the bread, Satan* came into
him. Then Jesus said to Judas, 'Do quickly what you want to
do.' 28 None of the other men who were sitting at the meal
understood this. They did not know why Jesus said this to
Judas. 29 Some of them thought that Jesus had asked Judas
to buy some things. Judas was going out to buy what they
needed for the festival*. That was what some of them thought.
Some of them thought that Jesus had asked Judas to give
some money to the poor people. That was because Judas kept
the bag of money on behalf of all of them.

30 Judas took the bread and then he went out immediately. And
it was night.

The new rule

31 When Judas had left, Jesus said, 'Now people will see how
great and how good the Son of Man is. And in him, they will
see how great and how good God is. 32 The Son will show
how great God is. Then God will take the Son to himself.
And God will show how great the Son is. And he will do that
immediately. 33 My children, I will be with you for only a short

time. You will look for me. But I tell you now what I told the
Jews*. You cannot go where I go now. 34 I give a new rule to
you. Love each other. You must love each other as I have loved
you. 35 By this, everyone will know that you are my disciples*.
They will know it, if you really love each other.'

36 Simon Peter asked him, 'Where will you go, LORD?' Jesus
replied, 'You cannot follow now where I will go. But you will
follow some time after this.' 37 Peter said, 'LORD, why can I not
follow you now? I would die for you.' 38 Jesus answered, 'You
say that you would die for me. But I am telling you what is
true. You will say that you do not know me. Before the first
bird sings, early in the morning, you will say it three times.'

14

Jesus is the way to the Father

1 Then Jesus said to them, 'Do not let yourselves be sad and
afraid. Believe God, and believe me also. 2 There are many
rooms in my Father's house. I would not tell you this if it was
not true. And I will go now so that I can prepare a place for
you. 3 After I have prepared a place for you, I will return. I will
take you so that you will be with me. So then you will be where
I am. 4 You know the way to the place where I will go.'

5 Thomas said to him, 'LORD, we do not know where you will go.
So how can we know the way to get there?' 6 Jesus answered,
'I am the way. I am what is true. And I am the life. Nobody
comes to the Father except by me. 7 If you really know me, you
will know my Father also. From this time, you do know him,
and you have seen him.'

8 Philip said, 'LORD, show the Father to us. That is all that we
need.' 9 Jesus answered, 'I have been with all of you for such a
long time. But still you do not seem to know me, Philip! Anyone
who has seen me has seen the Father. So why do you say,
"Show the Father to us"? 10 I am in the Father and the Father
is in me. You should believe that. The words that I say to you

do not come from me myself. But the Father, who lives in me,
is doing his work. 11 I am in the Father and the Father is in me.
Believe me when I say that. Or, if you do not believe my words,
believe because of my work. Believe because of the things
that I have done. 12 I am telling you what is true. Anyone who
believes me will do the same things as me. That person will do
the same things that I have done. Yes, he will do even greater
things than these, because I go to my Father. 13 Ask for things
in my name (because you are mine). If you ask anything in my
name, I will do it. So then the Son will show everyone how
great and how good the Father is. 14 If you ask me for anything
in my name, I will do it.'

Jesus promises God's Spirit

15 'If you love me, you will obey me. You will obey what I have
asked you to do. 16 I will ask the Father. And he will give to you
another Person who will help you. That Helper will stay with
you always. 17 He is the Spirit, who shows you true things. The
people who belong to this world cannot receive him. That is
because they cannot see him. They cannot know him. But you
know him because he stays with you. And he will be in you.
18 I will not let you remain alone, like children without parents.
I will come to you.'

19 'After a short time, the people who belong to this world will
not see me any longer. But you will see me. And because I live,
you will live also. 20 On that day, you will know that I am in my
Father. You will know that you are in me. And you will know
that I am in you. 21 Some people will listen to what I have told
them. And they will obey what I have said. It is those people
who love me. My Father will love everyone who loves me. And
I will love them and I will show myself to them.'

22 Then Judas (not Judas Iscariot) said, 'LORD, why will you
show yourself only to us? Why will you not show yourself also
to the people who belong to this world?'

23 Jesus replied, 'Anyone who loves me will obey my words. My
Father will love him. And my Father and I will come to him and
we will make our home with him. 24 Anyone who does not love
me will not obey my words. And these words that you hear are
not my own. No, these words come from the Father, who sent
me. 25 I have said these things to you while I am still with you.
26 But the Father will send the Holy (completely good) Spirit.
And it is he who will help you. He will come in my name. He
will teach you all things. And he will cause you to remember
everything that I have told you.'

27 'I will go away but I will cause a gift to stay with you. My
gift is that I will give you power* to be without trouble in your
minds and in your hearts*. In the same way that I myself have
this power*, I will cause you to have it also. My gift to you is
not like what this world gives. Do not let yourselves be sad or
afraid. 28 You heard me say to you, "I will go away, but I will
return to you." If you loved me, you would be happy because
of that. You would be happy because I go to the Father. And
he is greater than I am. 29 I have told you this now, before it
happens. So then, when it does happen, you will believe. 30 I will
not talk with you much more, because the ruler of this world
will come soon. He has no power* over me. 31 But the people
who belong to this world must learn about me. They must know
that I love the Father. And I do everything that he asks me to
do. I must show that to them. So get up, we must go.'

15

The branches must stay in the vine*

1 'I am the proper vine*, and my Father is the gardener. 2 Some
branches that are part of me may have no fruit on them. So,
my Father removes those branches. And he cuts short every
branch that does make fruit. He cleans all those branches, so
that they will make more fruit. 3 The words that I have spoken
to you have made you clean already. 4 Continue to live in me,
and I will continue to live in you. A branch cannot make fruit

by itself. It can make fruit only if it continues to be part of
the vine*. You are like that. You cannot make fruit unless you
continue to live in me.'

5 'I am the vine*, and you are the branches. You must remain in
me and I must remain in you. Only if you do that will you make
plenty of fruit. That is because you can do nothing without me.
6 If anyone does not remain in me, that person is like a dead
branch. The gardener will throw that branch away and it will
become dry. People take those dry branches and they throw
them into the fire. So, those dry branches burn. 7 You must
remain in me, and my words must remain in you. So then you
can ask for anything that you want. And God will do it for you.
8 If you make plenty of fruit, you will be my disciples*. You will
show how great and how good my Father is.'

9 'I have loved you as the Father has loved me. Continue to
know that I love you. 10 You must obey everything that I have
taught you. So, as a result, you will continue to know that
I love you. In the same way, I have obeyed everything that the
Father has asked me to do. So, as a result, I continue to know
that he loves me. 11 I have told you these things so that you
can be really happy. You can be happy in the same way that
I myself am happy. So you will be completely happy.'

12 'I tell you that you must do this: You must love each other, as
I have loved you. 13 A person really loves his friends if he dies
on behalf of them. Nobody could love anyone more than that.
14 And you are my friends, if you obey me. You must do what
I ask you to do. 15 A servant does not know what his master is
doing. So I do not call you servants any longer. But I have told
you everything that I have heard from my Father. So, I call
you friends. 16 You did not choose me, but I chose you. I chose
you for a purpose. You must go and you must make fruit. You
must make the kind of fruit that will continue. So, as a result,
the Father will give you anything that you ask him. If you ask
him in my name (because you are mine), he will give it to you.
17 This is what you must do: You must love each other.'

The world hates* the disciples*

18 'The people who belong to this world may hate* you. But
remember this: They hated* me before they hated* you. 19 If
you belonged to this world, this world's people would love
you. They would love you because you would belong with
them. But I chose you so that you would be separate from this
world's people. You do not belong with them, so they hate*
you. 20 Remember what I told you, "No slave is more important
than his master." If they have caused trouble for me, they will
cause trouble for you, too. But if they have obeyed my words,
they will obey your words, too. 21 They will do all these things
to you because of me. They do not know him who sent me.
That is why they will do these things.'

22 'I have come and I have spoken to them. If I had not done
that, they would not have done anything wrong. But now they
cannot say, "We have not done anything wrong." 23 Anyone
who hates* me hates* my Father also. 24 I did many great
things when I was with them. Nobody else ever did things like
that. If I had not done those things among them, they would
not have done anything wrong. But they have seen what I did.
And they have hated* me. And they have hated my Father
too. 25 But this had to happen. Their book of rules (the Old
Testament*) says, "They hated* me without any good reason."
And what it says had to happen.'

26 'But I will send the Helper to you from the Father. The Helper
is the Spirit who speaks only true things. He comes from the
Father. And he will speak about me. 27 You must speak about
me, too, because you have been with me from the beginning.'

16

1 'I have told you all this, so that nothing will cause you
to stop believing me. 2 People will send you away from the
synagogues*. There will be a time when people will kill you.
And they will even think that God has given them a duty to kill

you. 3They will do these things because they have never known
either the Father or me. 4But I have told you this so that you
will remember. When they begin to do these things, you will
remember. You will remember that I told you about them. I did
not tell you this before, because I was with you.'

The work of God's Spirit

5'Now I will go to him who sent me. But none of you asks me,
"Where will you go?" 6And now you are very sad, because of the
things that I have told you. 7But I am telling you what is true.
I will go away because it will be better for you. Unless I go away,
the Helper will not come to you. But if I do go away, I will send
him to you. 8When he comes, he will show things about this
world's people. He will show that they are wrong. They are wrong
about sin*. They are wrong about how to be right with God. They
are wrong about how God judges* people. 9They are wrong about
sin*, because they do not believe me. 10They are wrong about
how to be right with God, because I go to the Father. And you
will not see me any longer. 11They are wrong about how God
judges* people. They are wrong about that because God has
already decided to punish* the ruler of this world.'

12'I have many more things to tell you. But you are not strong
enough to know them now. 13But the Spirit, who shows you true
things, will come. And when he comes, he will be a guide to you.
He will cause you to know everything that is true. He will tell
you only what he hears. He will not speak his own words. He
will tell you about things that will happen after this time. 14He
will receive what I have to say. And he will tell it to you. In that
way, he will show how great and how good I am. 15Everything
that the Father has is mine. That is why I said, "The Spirit will
receive what I have to say. And then he will tell it to you." '

The disciples* will be sad first but after that they will be happy

16'After a short time, you will not see me any longer. But soon
after that, you will see me.' 17Some of his disciples* said to

each other, 'What does he mean? He says, "After a short time,
you will not see me any longer, but soon after that, you will
see me." And he says, "because I go to the Father." 18 What
does he mean by 'a short time'? We do not know what he is
talking about!'

19 Jesus knew that they wanted to ask him about this. So, he
said to them, 'I said, "After a short time, you will not see me
any longer. But soon after that, you will see me." Perhaps
you are asking each other about that. 20 I am telling you what
is true. You will cry and you will be sad. But the people who
belong to this world will be happy. First, you will be sad, but
soon after that, you will become happy instead. 21 While a
woman is giving birth to a baby, she is sad. She is sad at
that time because it is painful. But after the baby is born,
she is happy. She forgets the pain, because now she is so
happy. She is so happy because a person has been born into
the world.'

22 'It is like that for you. You are sad now. But I will see you
again, and you will be happy. You will be so happy. And nobody
will cause you to stop being happy. 23 On that day, you will not
ask me for anything. I am telling you what is true. The Father
will give you anything that you ask for in my name (because
you are mine). 24 Until now, you have not asked for anything
in my name. Ask, and you will receive. So then you will be
completely happy.'

25 'I have spoken to you with words and stories that are like
pictures. But there will be a time when I will not speak like
that any longer. Instead, I will speak clearly to you about the
Father. 26 On that day, you will ask in my name (because you
are mine). I am not saying that I will ask the Father on your
behalf. 27 No, because the Father himself loves you. He loves
you because you love me. He loves you because you believe.
You believe that I came from God. 28 I came from the Father,
and I came into the world. And now I will leave the world, and
I will return to the Father.'

29His disciples* said, 'Now you are speaking clearly. You are
not speaking with words that are like pictures! 30Now we are
sure that you know everything. You do not need to ask people
what they are thinking. Because of this, we believe that you
came from God.' 31Jesus answered them, 'You say that you
believe now. 32But it will happen very soon that all of you will
run away to your own homes. Yes, it is that time already. You
will leave me alone. But I am not really alone, because the
Father is with me. 33I have told you these things so that you
will be without trouble in your minds and in your hearts*.
You will be like that because you are united with me. In this
world, you will have trouble. But be strong! I have won! I have
destroyed the power* of this world.'

17

Jesus prays for himself

1After Jesus said this, he looked up to heaven*. He said,
'Father, it is the time. Show how great and how good your Son
is. So then I (the Son) can show how great and how good you
are. 2You gave to me (the Son) authority over all people. You
did this so that I (the Son) could cause people to live always.
I could cause all those people that you gave to me to live
always. 3And this is how they will live always. They will live
because they will know you. They will know you. And only you
really are God. And they will know Jesus Christ, whom you
have sent. 4I have finished the work that you gave to me to
do. And so, I have shown on the earth how great and how
good you are. 5Now, Father, show how great and how good
I am. Before the world began, I was with you. I was great and
powerful with you. Show again that I am great like that.'

Jesus prays for his disciples*

6'You gave some men to me out of the world. I have shown
them who you are. They were yours. You gave them to me,
and they have obeyed your words. 7Now they know about me.

Everything that you have given to me really comes from you.
They know that now. 8 I gave to them the words that you gave
to me. And they accepted those words. They know certainly
that I came from you. They believe that you sent me.'

9 'I pray for them. I am not praying for the people who belong
to this world. No, but I am praying for those people that you
have given to me. I am praying for them because they are
yours. 10 Everything that is mine is yours. And everything that
is yours is mine. And these people have shown how great
and how good I am. 11 Now, I will not remain in the world any
longer. I will come to you. But they are still in the world. Holy
(completely good) Father, keep them safe in your name (by
your own power*), that you gave to me. So then they can be
united in the same way that you and I are united. 12 While
I was with them, I kept them safe. I kept them safe in your
name (by your own power*), that you gave to me. I kept them
safe so that none of them went the wrong way, except one.
That was the man who had to go the wrong way. What the Old
Testament* says had to happen.'

13 'Now, I will come to you. But I am saying these things
while I am still in the world. I am saying them so that these
men can be completely happy in their hearts*. I want them
to become completely happy in the same way that I am
completely happy. 14 I have given your words to them. And the
world's people have hated* them because they do not belong
to the world. They do not belong to the world, in the same
way that I do not belong to the world. 15 I am not asking that
you will take them out of the world. But I want you to keep
them safe from him who is bad (the Devil*). So I am asking
you to do that. 16 They do not belong to the world, in the same
way that I do not belong to the world. 17 Make them separate
for yourself by your words, which are true. 18 I have sent them
into the world, in the same way that you sent me into the
world. 19 On behalf of them, I make myself separate, so that
I obey only you. So then they can become separate for you
also, by what is true.'

Jesus prays for everyone who will believe him

20 ‘I do not pray only for these people. I pray also for those
people who will believe me because of their words. 21 I pray
that all of them will be united. You, Father, are in me and I am
in you. I pray that they also will be united in us. So then the
world’s people will believe that you sent me. 22 I have given
to them the great and special gift that you gave to me. Now
they can be united in the same way that you and I are united.
23 I will be in them, and you will be in me. So then they can be
completely united. And, as a result, the world’s people will
know that you sent me. The world’s people will know that you
love them. You love them as you love me.’

24 ‘Father, you have given these people to me. And I want them
to be with me where I am. You made me great and powerful
because you loved me. You loved me before you made the
world. And I want these people to see how great and how
powerful I am. 25 Father, you always do what is right. The
world’s people do not know you, but I know you. And these
disciples* know that you have sent me. 26 I have shown them
what you are like. And I will continue to show them who you
are. So then they will love other people in the same way that
you love me. And so I can be in them.’

18

Soldiers take Jesus to the Chief Priest* (priests’* leader)

1 When Jesus had finished praying, he and his disciples* went
out. They went across the Kidron valley. On the other side,
there was a garden. Jesus and his disciples* went into it.
2 Judas, who sold Jesus to Jesus’ enemies*, knew the garden.
He knew it because Jesus and his disciples* had met there
often. 3 The most important priests* and the Pharisees* had
sent a group of soldiers and some officers to Judas. Judas led
these soldiers and officers to the garden. The soldiers had
long knives and they carried lights.

4 Jesus knew everything that would soon happen to him. So, he
went towards them. He asked them, 'Whom are you looking
for?' 5 They answered, 'Jesus, who comes from Nazareth.' Jesus
said, 'I am.'

Judas, who sold Jesus to Jesus' enemies*, was standing with
the soldiers. 6 When Jesus said to them, 'I am', the soldiers
moved away from him. They fell down to the ground. 7 So Jesus
asked them again, 'Whom are you looking for?' And they said,
'Jesus, who comes from Nazareth.' 8 Jesus said, 'I have told you
already that "I am" that person. So, if you are looking for me,
let these other men go.' 9 Jesus said this for a reason. Earlier,
he had said, 'I have lost none of those men that you gave to
me.' And what he had spoken earlier had to happen.

10 Simon Peter had a long knife. He lifted the knife and he
attacked the Chief Priest's* (priest's* leader's) servant. He cut
off the servant's right ear. The servant's name was Malchus.
11 Then Jesus said to Peter, 'Put your knife into the thing that
covers it! Let them take me. My Father has told me what must
happen to me. And I will obey him completely.'

12 The group of soldiers, with their captain and the Jews'*
officers, took Jesus and they tied him. 13 They led him first to
Annas, who was the father of Caiaphas's wife. Caiaphas was
the Chief Priest* (priests'* leader) that year. 14 It was Caiaphas
who had spoken to the Jews'* leaders some time before. He
had told them, 'It is better that one man should die on behalf
of all the people.'

Peter says that he does not know Jesus

15 Simon Peter and another disciple* followed Jesus. The Chief
Priest* (priests'* leader) knew that other disciple*. So, he went
with Jesus into the yard of the Chief Priest's* house. 16 But
Peter stayed outside by the gate. Then the other disciple*,
whom the Chief Priest* knew, went out again. He spoke to the
girl who was at the gate. Then he brought Peter inside. 17 The
girl who was at the gate spoke to Peter. She asked him, 'Are

you another of this man's (Jesus') disciples*?' Peter replied,
'No, I am not!' 18 It was cold. So the servants and the officers
were standing round a fire that they had made. They were
making themselves warm. Peter went to stand with them, so
that he could make himself warm too.

The Priests'* Leader asks Jesus some questions

19 The Chief Priest* (priests'* leader) asked Jesus about his
disciples*. He also asked Jesus about what Jesus taught.
20 Jesus answered him, 'I have spoken in public places so that
everyone could hear. I have always taught in synagogues*,
or in God's Great House (the temple), where all the Jews*
meet together. I have said nothing secretly. 21 So, you do not
need to ask me these questions. Ask the people who heard
me. Ask them what I said to them. They know what I said.'
22 When Jesus said this, one of the soldiers hit him on the face.
The soldier said, 'You must never speak to the Chief Priest*
(priests'* leader) like that!' 23 Jesus replied, 'If I said something
wrong, tell everyone about it. But if I said something true, you
should not have hit me.' 24 Then Annas sent Jesus, who still had
ropes* round his arms, to Caiaphas, the Chief Priest* (priests'*
leader).

Peter says again that he does not know Jesus

25 Simon Peter was still standing there (by the fire) so that he
could make himself warm. The other people there said to him,
'We think that you are one of that man's disciples*.' But Peter
said, 'No, I am not.'

26 A servant of the priests'* leader belonged to the same
family* as the man whose ear Peter had cut off. This servant
said to Peter, 'I am sure that I saw you in the garden with him
(Jesus).' 27 Again, Peter said, 'No.' And immediately the first
bird sang, early in the morning.

Pilate, the Roman* ruler, asks Jesus some questions

28 The Jews* led Jesus from Caiaphas's house to the Roman*
ruler's big house (called the Praetorium). It was early in the
morning. The Jews'* leaders themselves did not go into the
house because they wanted to be 'clean'. They wanted to eat
the Passover* meal.

29 So Pilate went outside to meet them. He asked them, 'What
do you say that this man has done wrong?' 30 They replied, 'We
would not have brought him to you if he had done nothing
wrong.' 31 So Pilate said to them, 'You yourselves take him away.
You judge* him by your own rules.' The Jews* replied, 'We do
not have authority to kill anyone.' 32 This happened because of
what Jesus had said earlier. Jesus had told them how he would
die. So, what he had said had to happen.

33 Pilate returned into his big house (the Praetorium). He
told Jesus that he must come to him. Pilate asked Jesus, 'Are
you the king of the Jews*?' 34 Jesus said, 'Is that your own
idea, or have other people spoken to you about me?' 35 Pilate
replied, 'I am not a Jew*! It was your own people and their
most important priests* who brought you to me. What have
you done?' 36 Jesus said, 'My kingdom* does not belong to this
world. If it did, my people would have fought. They would have
fought so that the Jews* could not take me. No, my kingdom
is from another place.' 37 Pilate said to him, 'So do you mean
that you really are a king?' Jesus answered, 'It is you are using
the word "king". I was born and I came into the world for only
one purpose. I came to tell people what is true. Everyone who
loves all true things hears my voice.' 38 Pilate said, 'I do not
know if anything is really true.'

Then Pilate went out again to the Jews. He said to them, 'This
man seems to have done nothing wrong. I have no reason
to punish him. 39 But every year we do something for you
Jews. We let one man go free from the prison at the time of
your Passover. Do you want me to let the king of the Jews go

free?' 40They shouted their answer, 'No, we do not want him!
We want Barabbas!' (Barabbas was a man who had robbed
people.)

19

1Then Pilate told the soldiers that they should take Jesus
outside. He told them that they should hit Jesus many times
with a whip*.

2The soldiers took some branches that had sharp points all
over them. They made the branches into a circle that they put
on Jesus' head. Then they took a dark red coat (like a king's
coat) and they put that on him. 3The soldiers came to him and
they hit him with their hands. While they were hitting him,
they said to him, 'Hello, great King of the Jews*!'

4Pilate went outside once more. He said to the crowd, 'Look,
I will bring him (Jesus) out here to you. So now you will know
that I cannot find any reason to punish* him.' 5So Jesus came
out, with the circle of branches on his head. He was wearing
the dark red coat. Pilate said to them, 'Look. Here is the man!'
6When the most important priests* and the officers saw
Jesus, they shouted, 'Kill him! Kill him on a cross*!' Pilate said
to them, 'You take him yourselves, and you kill him on a cross.
I find no reason why anyone should punish* him.' 7The Jews*
answered, 'We have a rule. That rule says that he must die.
He must die because he said, "I am the Son of God".'

8When Pilate heard that, he was even more afraid. 9He
returned into the big house (the Praetorium). He asked Jesus,
'Where are you from?' But Jesus did not answer. 10Pilate said
to him, 'Are you refusing to speak to me? Remember that
I have authority. I can let you go free, or I can let them
kill you on a cross*.' 11Jesus answered, 'You could have no
authority against me unless God had given it to you. So, the
man who sent me to you has done a worse thing. That man has
done a worse thing than you have done.' 12From that moment,
Pilate tried to let Jesus go free. But the Jews* shouted

back, 'If you let him go, you are not Caesar's* friend. Nobody should say that he himself is a king. Anyone who says that is Caesar's enemy*!'

13When Pilate heard those words, he brought Jesus outside.
Pilate sat down on a special seat, where he judged*. The seat
was in a place called 'Gabbatha' in the Jews'* language. There
were large flat stones there, which covered the ground. 14It
was about 6 in the morning on the day when they prepared
the Passover* meal. Pilate said to the Jews*, 'Here is your
king!' 15But they shouted, 'Take him away! Take him away! Kill
him on a cross*!' Pilate asked them, 'Do you want me to kill
your king on a cross?' The most important priests* answered,
'Caesar* is the only ruler that we call king.' 16Then Pilate gave
Jesus to them, so that they could kill him on a cross*.

They fix Jesus to a cross*

17Jesus went out to the place called 'The Place of the Skull'*.
This place is called 'Golgotha' in the Jews'* language. He was
carrying his own cross*.

18They fixed him to the cross* with nails (short, sharp pieces
of metal) and then they lifted the cross up. They put two other
men on crosses with him, one on each side of him. Jesus was
between them.

19Pilate wrote a notice, and then he put it on the cross*. It
said: 'Jesus from Nazareth, the King of the Jews'*. 20The place
where they put Jesus on the cross* was near to the city. So,
many of the Jews* read this notice. They could read it because
Pilate had written the words three times. He had written it in
the Jews'* language and in the languages called Roman and
Greek. 21The Jews'* most important priests* said to Pilate, 'Do
not write: the King of the Jews*. Instead, write: This man said,
"I am the King of the Jews*".' 22Pilate answered, 'I will not
change what I have written.'

23After the soldiers had put Jesus on the cross*, they took
his clothes. They made them into 4 parts, one part for each

soldier. Also, they took his coat, which somebody had made
from one piece of cloth. It was not several pieces of cloth that
somebody had put together. 24 So they said to each other, 'We
will not tear it. Instead, we will play a game. The person who
wins the game will have the coat.' This happened because the
Old Testament* says:

'Each of them took some of my clothes.

They played a game to win what I was wearing.'

So, that is what the soldiers did.

25 Some women stood near to Jesus while he was on the cross*.
They were his mother, his mother's sister - Mary the wife of
Cleopas - and Mary Magdalene (Mary from Magdala). 26 Jesus
saw his mother. Also he saw the disciple* that he loved. That
disciple* was standing near Jesus' mother. So Jesus said to
his mother, 'Woman, here is your son.' 27 Then he said to the
disciple*, 'Here is your mother.' From that time, the disciple*
took her to live in his own home.

Jesus dies

28 Now Jesus had done everything that God had sent him into
the world to do. Jesus knew this. So, because of what it says
in the Old Testament*, he said, 'I want a drink.' What it says
in the Old Testament* had to happen. 29 There was a pot full
of cheap wine* there. So the soldiers put a cloth into the
wine*. They fixed the cloth to the end of a branch. The branch
was from a plant called hyssop. Then they lifted the cloth
up to Jesus' mouth. 30 Jesus drank the wine*. Then he said,
'I have finished it.' Then he bent his head down and he let his
spirit* go.

A soldier puts a spear* into Jesus

31 It was a Friday - the day when the Jews* prepared
themselves for the Sabbath* day. And that Sabbath* day was
a very important one. The Jews* did not want the dead bodies

to stay on the cross* on the Sabbath* day. So they asked
Pilate to speak to the soldiers. The soldiers would break the
legs of the men who were on the crosses. Then they could take
the dead bodies down from the crosses.

32 So the soldiers went there. And they broke the legs of the
two other men who were on the crosses* next to Jesus. 33 But
when they came to Jesus, he was dead already. They saw that
he was dead. So they did not break his legs. 34 But one of the
soldiers put a spear* into Jesus' side. Immediately, blood and
water came out. 35 The man who saw this has spoken about it.
What he says is true. He knows that it really happened. He
says this so that you can believe. 36 This happened because of
what the Old Testament* says. It says:

> 'Nobody will break any of his bones.'

And what the Old Testament* says must happen. 37 And, in
another place, the Old Testament* says:

> 'People will look at the man whose body they have made a hole in.'

Joseph buries Jesus

38 After that, a man asked Pilate if he could take Jesus' dead
body away. The man was called Joseph. He came from the
town called Arimathea. He was one of Jesus' disciples*, but
that was a secret. It was a secret because he was afraid of the
Jews'* leaders. Pilate told Joseph that he could take the dead
body. So Joseph went there and he took it away. 39 Nicodemus,
the man who, earlier, had visited Jesus at night, went with
Joseph. Nicodemus brought about 100 pounds of spices* called
myrrh and aloes. 40 The two men covered Jesus' dead body
with these spices*. And they put long pieces of cloth round it
again and again. That is how the Jews* prepare a dead body
before they bury it. 41 There was a garden at the place where
they killed Jesus on the cross*. In that garden there was a new
tomb*, where nobody had ever put a dead person. 42 The next

day was the Jews'* Sabbath*, and this tomb* was near. So,
they put Jesus there.

20

The tomb* is empty

1 Early on the first day of the week, Mary from Magdala went
to the tomb*. It was still dark. She saw that someone had
removed the big stone from the way into the tomb*. 2 So she
ran to where Simon Peter was. He was with the other disciple*,
the one that Jesus loved. She said to them, 'They have taken
the LORD out of the tomb*. And we do not know where they
have put him!'

3 So Peter and the other disciple* started to go to the tomb*.
4 Both of them were running. But the other disciple* ran
faster than Peter ran. So he reached the tomb* first. 5 He
bent himself down and he looked inside the tomb*. He saw
the long pieces of cloth that were lying there. But he did
not go in. 6 Simon Peter had run behind the other disciple*.
When Peter arrived, he went into the tomb*. He saw the
long pieces of cloth that were lying there. 7 Also, he saw the
piece of cloth that had been round Jesus' head. This was not
in the same place as the other pieces of cloth. Someone had
put it carefully in a separate place. 8 Then the other disciple*,
who had reached the tomb* first, went inside also. He saw
and he believed. 9 They still did not understand what the Old
Testament* says. It says that Jesus had to become alive again.
After he had died, he had to become alive again.

Jesus appears to Mary from Magdala

10 Then the disciples* returned to their homes. 11 But Mary
stood outside the tomb*. She was crying. While she cried, she
bent herself down to look inside the tomb*. 12 She saw two
angels* who were wearing white clothes. They were sitting
where Jesus' dead body had been. One angel* was sitting

where Jesus' head had been. The other angel* was sitting where his feet had been.

13They asked her, 'Woman, why are you crying?' 14She replied,
'They have taken away my LORD. And I do not know where they have put him.' When she had said this, she turned round. And she saw a man who was standing there. It was Jesus, but she did not recognise him.
15Jesus said to her, 'Woman, why are you crying? Whom are you looking for?' She thought that he was the gardener. So she said, 'Sir, if you have carried him away, please tell me. Tell me where you have put him. Then I will take him away.'

16Jesus said to her, 'Mary.' She turned towards him and she said in the Jews'* language, 'Rabboni!' (This means 'Teacher'.)
17Jesus said, 'Do not hold on to me because I have not gone up to the Father yet. But go to my brothers (the disciples*). Tell them, "I go up to my Father. And he is your Father. He is my
God, and he is your God." '
18Mary from Magdala went to the disciples*. She said to them, 'I have seen the LORD!' Then she told them what he had said to her.

Jesus appears to his disciples*

19On the evening of that same day, the first day of the week, the disciples* were all together. They had locked the doors of the room because they were afraid of the Jews'* leaders. Then Jesus came and he stood among them. He said to them, 'Be
without trouble in your minds and in your hearts*.'
20After he had said this, he showed them his hands and his side. The disciples* were very, very happy when they saw the LORD.
21Jesus said again, 'Be without trouble in your minds and in your hearts*. As the Father sent me, in the same way I am
sending you.'
22When he had said this, he caused air from his
mouth to blow on them. And he said, 'Receive God's Spirit.
23If you forgive* a person's sins*, God will forgive* them too. If you do not forgive* them, God will not forgive* them.'

Jesus shows himself to Thomas

24 One of the 12 disciples* was called Thomas. He was not
with the other disciples when Jesus came. (Thomas was also
called 'the Twin'*.) 25 So the other disciples* told him, 'We have
seen the Lord.' But Thomas said to them, 'I will never believe
that unless I myself see him. I want to see the marks of the
nails* in his hands. I want to put my finger where the nails*
were. I want to put my hand into the hole in his side. I will not
believe unless I do those things.'

26 Eight days after that, the disciples* were in the house again,
and Thomas was with them. They had locked the door. But Jesus
came and he stood among them. He said, 'Be without trouble
in your minds and in your hearts*.' 27 Then he said to Thomas,
'Put your finger in here. Look at my hands. Put your hand in my
side. Do not refuse to believe, but instead, believe.' 28 Thomas
answered him, 'My Lord, and my God!' 29 Jesus said to him, 'You
believe because you have seen me. Other people have not seen,
but they do believe. And God will be good to those people.'

The purpose of this book

30 Jesus did many other miracles* while the disciples* were
with him. I have not written about them in this book. 31 But
I have written about these things, so that you will be able to
believe. You will be able to believe that Jesus is the Christ*,
the Son of God. And when you believe, you will be able to live.
You will be able to live because of who he is.

21

Jesus shows himself to the disciples* again

1 After that, Jesus showed himself to the disciples* again. They
were by Lake Tiberias. This is how it happened. 2 Simon Peter,
Thomas the Twin*, and Nathanael (who came from Cana in
Galilee) were together. They were with the sons of Zebedee

(James and John) and two other disciples*. 3Simon Peter said
to the other disciples*, 'I am going to catch fish.' They replied,
'We will come with you.' So they went out and they got into the
boat. But they caught nothing during that night.

4Early in the morning, Jesus was standing on the shore.
But the disciples* did not know that it was Jesus. 5Then
Jesus asked them, 'Friends, have you caught any fish?' They
answered, 'No!' 6He said, 'Throw your net* out on the right
side of the boat. If you do that, you will catch some fish.' So
they threw the net* out. Then they caught so many fish that
they could not pull the net* into the boat.

7The disciple* that Jesus loved said to Peter, 'It is the LORD!'
When Simon Peter heard him say, 'It is the LORD', he put on
his coat. (He was wearing only a very few clothes.) Then Peter
jumped into the water. 8The other disciples* followed him in
the boat. They pulled the net* that was full of fish behind
them. They were not far from the shore. It was about 100
metres away. 9When they came to the shore, they saw a red
fire there. Some fish were lying on the fire. There was some
bread there, too. 10Jesus said to them, 'Bring some of the fish
that you have just caught.'

11Simon Peter got into the boat and he pulled the net* on to
the shore. It was full of big fish. There were 153 fish. There
were so many fish, but the net* did not tear. 12Jesus said to
them, 'Come and eat breakfast.' None of the disciples* was
brave enough to ask him, 'Who are you?' They knew that it
was the LORD. 13So Jesus went and he got the bread. Then he
gave it to them. And he did the same with the fish.

14This was the third time that Jesus showed himself to the
disciples*. After Jesus had died, he had become alive again.
And this was the third time that he showed himself to them.

Jesus talks to Peter

15When they had finished eating, Jesus spoke to Simon Peter.
He said, 'Simon, son of John, do you love me more than these?'

Peter answered, 'Yes LORD, you know that I love you.' Jesus
said to him, 'Feed my lambs (young sheep).'

16 Jesus asked him a second time, 'Simon, son of John, do you
love me?' Peter answered, 'Yes LORD, you know that I love you.'
Jesus said to him, 'Look after* my sheep*.' 17 Jesus asked him
a third time, 'Simon, son of John, do you love me?' Peter was
sad because Jesus asked him a third time, 'Do you love me?'
So he said to Jesus, 'LORD, you know everything. You know
that I do love you!' Jesus said to him, 'Look after* my sheep*.
18 I am telling you what is true. When you were young, you got
yourself ready. And you went to any place that you wanted to
visit. But when you are old, it will be different. You will hold
out your arms and someone else will tie you. Then they will
take you where you do not want to go.' 19 Jesus was speaking
about how Peter would die. It would show how great God is.
Then Jesus said to Peter, 'Follow me.'

20 Peter turned round. He saw another disciple*. It was the
disciple* that Jesus loved. This disciple* was following them.
He was the man who had been very near to Jesus at the
supper. This disciple* had asked Jesus, 'LORD, who will sell you
to your enemies*?' 21 When Peter saw this disciple*, he asked
Jesus, 'LORD, what will happen to him?' 22 Jesus answered him,
'Perhaps I might want him to live on the earth until I return.
But it does not matter to you. You must follow me!'

23 Then people began to talk about these words that Jesus had
said. People who believed Jesus began to have a wrong idea
about this disciple*. They thought that this disciple* would not
die. But Jesus did not say, 'He will not die.' Instead, he said,
'Perhaps I might want him to live until I return. But it does not
matter to you.' 24 This is the disciple* who spoke about these
things. This is the disciple* who wrote them down. And what
he said is true. We know that.

25 Jesus did many other things also. If people wrote down all
those things, there would be many, many books. I do not think
that the whole world could contain all those books.

WORD LIST

ancestor ancestors are people centuries ago that your grandparents' grandparents were born to.

angel spirit* being (a being is a person or animal that is alive). Good angels come from heaven*. They are God's servants and they bring messages from God to people.

baptise to put a person into water to show that he or she wants to obey God.

Baptist a man who baptises* people.

breathe to get air in through the mouth.

Caesar Caesar was the ruler of all the countries that the Romans* had beaten. He ruled from Rome city itself (the capital of the country that we call Italy now).

Christ the special man that God sent to save his people.

circumcise to cut off the skin that covers the end of a boy's or a man's sex part.

cross a piece of wood that someone has fastened across another piece. People put Jesus on a cross to kill him.

Dedication when you give something to God for him to use.

Devil the leader and the worst of the bad angels*; God's enemy, who is also called Satan. A devil (or demon) is a bad spirit* that is the Devil's servant.

Didymus the other name of one of Jesus' 12 special disciples*; Didymus means 'the Twin'. Twins are two children who were born at the same time to the same mother.

disciple a person who believes and obeys Jesus; someone who wants to learn from Jesus and to be like him.

donkey an animal like a small horse.

enemy someone that wants to hurt or attack you; someone that wants to do bad things to you.

family family included father, mother and children; it might also include grandfathers and those who had been born before them. The 12 families of Israel included everyone who belonged to Israel's people.

festival (also called feast) - a special time when Israel's people came to worship* God at Jerusalem. They remembered something that God had done on their behalf. There were several festivals during every year.

Festival of Tabernacles this festival* continued for a week. The people built houses from branches and they lived in these small houses during the festival*. This helped them to remember what God had done many years before. A long time before, their ancestors* had left Egypt and they had lived in houses like this.

forgive when God (or another person) chooses to forget the wrong things that we do.

Greeks people who come from the country called Greece. When Jesus lived on the earth, Greek people lived in many places outside Greece.

harvest the time when people bring in the fruits and other food from the farmers' fields.

hate to strongly or completely not like something or someone. To hate is the opposite of when you love something or someone.

heart the place deep inside a person where they feel things. For example, they may feel happy or sad, or brave or afraid.

heaven the place beyond the earth where God and Jesus Christ live.

Holy One the special person that God has chosen; another way to say 'Messiah'*.

Jew someone who is born from Abraham, Isaac, Jacob and their children. The ancestors* of the Jews* were first called Israelites (Israel's people). They were the sons of Jacob (Israel). Many years after that, God sent almost all of the Israelites away. Only the people from Judah's family* group remained. So they started to be called Jews.

judge to say what is right or wrong, good or bad; also to say how to punish* people who have done wrong things.

kingdom a place where a king rules, or the people and things that he rules over.

lamb young sheep. John the Baptist* called Jesus 'God's Lamb'. Israel's people killed young sheep so that God would forgive* their sins*. Jesus Christ was God's Lamb, who came to die on our behalf. He came to save us from sin*.

Levite a man from the family* of Levi. Levi was one of the sons of Jacob. We can read about this family* in Exodus and Leviticus, and in 1 Chronicles 23:28-32. Levites worked in God's Great House (the temple), but they were not priests*.

look after be good to; keep safe, as a shepherd* keeps his sheep safe.

Lord master; another name for God. It means that he is greater than everyone else.

messenger a person who brings a message.

Messiah the special person that God had chosen to save his people - Jesus Christ. The Messiah was a man that God would send to save Israel's people. They thought that he would come to send away the Roman* soldiers. They thought that he would be a king like David. They believed that he would make sick people well too. The prophets* had said that he would be born in David's city, Bethlehem.

miracle a great thing, like when a dead person becomes alive again or a sick person becomes well; a thing that only God can do.

money-changers these people bought and sold coins.

mud material from the ground and water that you have mixed.

nail a short, sharp piece of metal.

net a big bag with small holes in it; people use it to catch fish.

Old Testament the first part of the Bible; it describes events before Jesus' life on earth. This was the only part of the Bible (called the Scriptures) that the people had during Jesus' life on earth.

olive a tree with small fruits (or the fruits themselves) that people used to make oil. They burned the oil to give them light. They used it in other ways too.

palm a tree with big leaves.

Passover the time (festival*) each year when the Jews* remembered how God had brought them out of Egypt. He told them that they must put a young sheep's blood on the wood round their doors. So then the angel* that killed all the oldest sons of Egypt's people passed over the houses of Israel's people.

Pharisees a group of Jews* who were very careful to obey all the rules that God had given to Moses. They had many other rules also, that they thought were very important. They did not like people who did not agree with them.

power what someone is able to do, or what someone has authority to do.

priest a man from Levi's family* group, who worked in God's Great House (the temple) in Jerusalem.

prophet person who speaks words from God. In the Old* Testament, the prophets often spoke about what would happen in future times.

punish to hurt someone, or to cause trouble for them, because they have done wrong things.

Roman a person who came from Rome city (in Italy). When Jesus lived on the earth, the Romans had a very powerful army. They ruled Israel and many other countries.

rope long thin piece of material; people use it to tie things together.

Sabbath the seventh day of the week. God told Israel's people that they must rest on this day.

Satan the bad spirit* who wants to be God. He is the ruler of bad angels* and of everything that is bad. He is the enemy of Christians. Another name for Satan is the Devil.

sheep Jesus uses this word to mean people that he wants to be good to.

shepherd person who keeps sheep safe.

sin what makes us sinful*. Sin has authority over every person who is born into this world. When we come to Christ, he stops sin's authority over us. Sins are the wrong things that people do.

sinful when a person does not love or obey God. All people are born sinful, with their spirits* dead to God. As a result, they cannot really know God or be friends with him. Sinful things (sins) are the wrong things that sinful people do.

skull bone in head that gives it its shape.

Solomon's Porch a part outside the Great House of God. People often met together there to listen while someone taught them. Only the priests* could go into the Great House of God. Other people remained outside.

spear a long piece of wood or metal that has a sharp point at the end. Roman* soldiers used spears when they fought against enemies.

spices oils or powders that have a lovely smell.

spirit the part of a person that will always be alive. It will be alive even after their body is dead. Our spirit is the part of us that receives God's Spirit. There are good spirits, like God's Spirit and his angels*. And there are bad spirits, like the Devil (God's enemy) and his angels*.

synagogue a building in each town, where Jews* met to pray. They also met to study and to worship* God.

thirsty a thirsty person wants or needs a drink.

tomb a place where people bury dead bodies. Jesus' tomb was a big hole in the rock.

trust to believe that someone will do the right thing.

twin twins are two children who were born at the same time to the same mother.

vine a kind of plant that has many small, sweet fruits called grapes. People make wine* from grapes.

wheat a kind of plant; people make bread with the seeds.

whip something to hit people and animals with; people made it out of very long and very thin pieces of material with something sharp at the end. People hit a person with it to punish* them.

wild place a place where people do not usually live.

wine a drink that people make from small, sweet fruits called grapes. It contains alcohol.

worship to love and to thank someone (God) more than anyone else.

www.ingramcontent.com/pod-product-compliance
Ingram Content Group UK Ltd.
Pitfield, Milton Keynes, MK11 3LW, UK
UKHW020236250726
13967UKWH00001B/390